Y0-BPW-848

No. 155. A Decorative Monogram for a Bedspread

Old-Fashioned Monogramming for Needleworkers

by
THE PRISCILLA PUBLISHING CO.

DOVER PUBLICATIONS, INC.
NEW YORK

NOTE: The original Priscilla illustration numbers refer to patterns available by mail order when this volume was first published in 1916. We do not have copies of these patterns and the Priscilla Company has been out of business over a half-century; however, we have left the numbers in place as there are references in the text.

As alternatives, we suggest several Dover volumes of alphabet patterns. Many of these designs are remarkably close to the old Priscilla illustrations and the same techniques can easily be applied.

ALPHABET IRON-ON TRANSFER PATTERNS, Rita Weiss (23298-0) $1.50

CHARTED MONOGRAMS FOR NEEDLEPOINT AND CROSS-STITCH, Rita Weiss (23555-6) $1.75

DECORATIVE ALPHABETS FOR NEEDLEWORKERS, CRAFTSMEN & ARTISTS, Carol Belanger Grafton (24175-0) $4.00

NEEDLEWORK ALPHABETS AND DESIGNS, Blanche Cirker (23159-3) $2.25

VICTORIAN ALPHABETS, MONOGRAMS AND NAMES FOR NEEDLEWORKERS from Godey's Lady's Book and Peterson's Magazine, Rita Weiss (23072-4) $3.50

Published in Canada by General Publishing Company, Ltd., 30 Lesmill Road, Don Mills, Toronto, Ontario.

Published in the United Kingdom by Constable and Company, Ltd., 10 Orange Street, London WC2H 7EG.

This Dover edition, first published in 1985, is an unabridged republication of the work first published by The Priscilla Publishing Company, Boston, Mass., in 1916 under the title *The Priscilla Monogram and Initial Book: A Collection of Various Styles of Initials and Monograms with Details of Stitches and Expert Advice on Marking Linen*, compiled and edited by Ethelyn J. Morris.

Manufactured in the United States of America
Dover Publications, Inc., 31 East 2nd Street, Mineola, N.Y. 11501

Library of Congress Cataloging in Publication Data

Priscilla monogram and initial book.
 Old-fashioned monogramming for needleworkers.

 Previously published as: The Priscilla monogram and initial book.
 Reprint. Originally published: Boston : Priscilla Pub. Co., 1916.
 1. Embroidery. 2. Monograms. 3. Initials.
I. Priscilla Publishing Co. II. Title.
TT773.P75 1985   746.44'041   84-21036
ISBN 0-486-24786-4 (pbk.)

INITIALS AND MONOGRAMS

THEIR USES IN MARKING LINEN

THE NECESSARY STITCHES

No. 112. SIZES, ⅞, 2, 3, AND 4 INCHES

S in all forms of embroidery, the marking of linen with embroidered monograms or initials has many variations, and there are many avenues of choice open to the worker, both in the style of marking to be adopted and the manner of embroidering, but there is one fixed rule to be obeyed if even a small degree of success is to be enjoyed, and that is, the work must be beautifully done with the proper materials and with neatness.

In order to do good monogram work it is not absolutely necessary to use very fine threads. If the threads are laid in the right direction and very close together over a good underlay, the work will seem quite as fine as if it is done with a very fine thread. If the padding is firm and kept well within the outline, and the overlay is placed with stitches close together, the lines will be straight and true and unbroken. On very fine fabrics a fine thread and needle must be used, and if any eyelet-work enters into the design, this must be done with fine thread.

One very important matter, in fact essential necessity, is to have

FIG. 1. SIMPLE OUTLINE

the designs well stamped or drawn so that all the lines are perfectly true.

While all the stitches shown on these pages are not absolutely necessary to know before one can embroider monograms, in fact only a few of the very simple stitches are commonly used, it is well to be familiar with many styles, and these details will serve as a reference when one wishes to introduce some fancy bit of stitchery into her marking.

The *simple outline* shown in Fig. 1 is worked from left to right over a single stamped line, putting the needle forward a short distance and bringing it up exactly at the end of the last stitch, and taking care to keep the stitches regular. The thread is always kept on the same side of the line, but it may be above or below as preferred; some workers prefer one method and some the other. The upper method, with the thread brought below the line, allows each stitch to stand out prominently and also shows the twist of the thread, while the other way forms a more un-

FIG. 2. DOUBLE OUTLINE

twisted cordlike appearance preferred by some.

To obtain a heavier effect and one which is often very pleasing, the *double outline* is used. This is made in the same manner as the simple outline, except that the needle is brought up at the end of the next to the last stitch, thus making the stitches longer and partially overlapping.

The outline which is most used in monogram and initial work, and in all French embroidery, is the *satin outline* shown in Fig. 3.

FIG. 3. SATIN OUTLINE

It consists of a series of short regular stitches taken at right angles to the line of stamping, which has previously been run with a single line of padding. To obtain a heavier effect the line may first be outlined and then covered with satin-stitches, or the stitches may be worked over a small cord or coarse thread, held with the left hand along the stamped line. Care must be taken to hold the padding thread not too loosely nor too tightly, for in either case the result will be a sad wobbly line.

Another important stitch, in fact the most important stitch, in monogram work is the padded *satin-stitch*. The space to be covered is first filled with close, firm darning-stitches running lengthwise of the space and padded higher in the middle than on the sides, then these are covered with very regular smooth satin-stitches taken across the space from side to side. This stitch may be made from right to left (as illustrated) or from left to right as seems easier and more convenient to the worker.

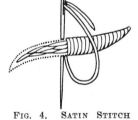

FIG. 4. SATIN STITCH

The *voided satin-stitch* is made in exactly the same manner, working two sections side by side. Often a space is voided only a part of the way, then the two portions converge into one. This stitch is especially useful in working broad spaces which seem too wide for a single stitch.

Buttonholing may be padded or not as the case seems to demand, and its entire success depends upon its firmness and regularity. Even when not padded it is well to run a row of short stitches along the outer line of stamping. It is worked from left to right, holding the thread down with the left thumb while a stitch is taken across the

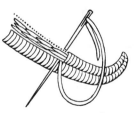

FIG. 5. VOIDED SATIN STITCH

3

space to be covered, keeping the needle always pointed towards the worker. When the loop is released by the thumb and the thread is drawn up, a purling is formed on the outer edge of the space. This stitch is useful and necessary in cut-work and on outer edges from which the linen is to be cut away.

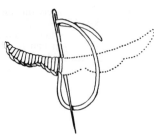

FIG. 6. BUTTONHOLING

The *Balkan stitch,* which is nice for filling broad spaces when padding is not necessary, is made by bringing the thread up on the left line, then inserting the needle on the right line and taking a downward slanting stitch, bringing it up in the middle between the two lines and above the loose thread. The thread

FIG. 7
BALKAN STITCH

is caught down with a short stitch and the needle is again brought up on the left ready for the next stitch.

While *eyelets* are not often essential in monogram embroidery, they are sometimes introduced with pleasing results, and to be perfectly satisfactory they should be worked with fine thread and a fine needle. Run a thread around the line of stamping, run two threads if the material is sheer or reamy, letting the stitches of the second row alternate with those of the first row, then slit the eyelet, roll back the edges and shape with a stiletto and whip over and over with short regular stitches. A shaded eyelet, one which is heavier on one side, is padded between the double lines, and otherwise worked in the ordinary way.

The *seed-stitch* is quite important and also very simple. Its chief requirement is that it must be regular. It consists of one, two, or more short stitches taken over and over at regular intervals to fill a space. The work progresses from right to left, keeping the needle pointed towards the left. Sometimes the stitches are grouped in clusters to form certain patterns over the surface. The lines confining the seed-stitch may be in plain outline or in satin outline as the conditions seem to require.

When something more than a single line and less than a satin-covered space is desired, a loose, open stitch such as the *herringbone-stitch* is very use-

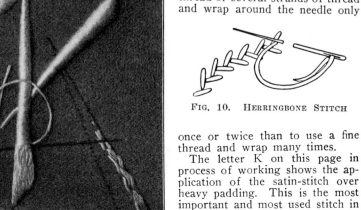

SHOWING PROCESS OF WORKING JAPANESE INITIAL, No. 114
SIZES, ⅞, 1, 1½, 2, 2½, 3, AND 4 INCHES

ful. Worked over a single line the stitches diverge first on one side and then on the other, letting the end of each stitch be covered by the end of the preceding stitch.

French knots are made when quick spots heavier than seed-stitches are desired or when one wishes to fill a space with an uneven

FIG. 9. SEED STITCH

effect. Bring the thread out on the right side of the linen, then, holding it with the left hand, wrap once or several times around the needle, keeping the point of the needle away from the linen; insert the needle close by where it was brought up and hold the thread taut or place the left thumb over the knot while the needle is being carried through. It is well to use hoops and a frame if many French knots are to be made, so that both hands will be free to manipulate the thread. To make large French knots it is better to use a heavy thread or several strands of thread and wrap around the needle only

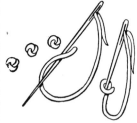

FIG. 10. HERRINGBONE STITCH

once or twice than to use a fine thread and wrap many times.

The letter K on this page in process of working shows the application of the satin-stitch over heavy padding. This is the most important and most used stitch in monogram work, and one which should be thoroughly mastered before attempting any important marking. Further information along this line is given under the subject of padding, which treats of the underlying principles of good monogram work.

Cross-stitch, usually worked in colors, consists of two short stitches crossing at right angles. The top stitches should all run in the same direction to give the finished work a smooth, regular appearance. Each cross may be finished as the work progresses as in the line detail or, when a space is to be filled with a number of crosses of the same color, it may seem more expeditious to first put in all the underlying threads of a row and go back, putting in the top threads. For this stitch a fairly coarse thread is usually employed or several fine threads together in the needle.

FIG. 11. FRENCH KNOTS

Sometimes cross-stitch designs are stamped on the linen and worked by the stamping, but the more exact method and the one followed by particular workers is to use an open canvas as a guide, working the crosses over the threads of the canvas, then removing the canvas thread by thread. If the work is to be done on

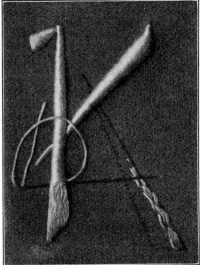

FIG. 8. EYELETS

a regular weave fabric, such as Hardanger cloth, Java canvas, or a coarse linen of regular weave, the crosses may easily be made directly on the material, counting the threads to get the design properly placed.

FIG. 12. CROSS STITCH

In making a *woven bar* across a space from which the linen is to be cut, carry two threads across the space, fasten securely in the edge and weave over and under the two threads, keeping the weaving of regular tension. Before the linen is cut of course the edges must be run and buttonholed or else worked very closely over and over as in satin outline or after the manner of an eyelet.

Buttonholed bars or *Italian cut-work,* also called "ladder stitch," can be used in spaces similar to those requiring woven bars. The edges are run and buttonholed and then the bars made by carrying several threads across from side to side and covering with close buttonholing, keeping the bars at regular intervals. If preferred the bars may be made first and the edges worked afterwards, covering the ends of the bars. (See detail of work on letter P.) The linen is cut from beneath the bars.

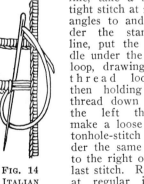

FIG. 13. WOVEN BAR

Cat-stitch is worked from left to right, keeping the needle always pointed towards the left. The stitches are taken above and below, alternately, on imaginary or real parallel lines, letting the stitches touch the preceding ones for a close effect or having them separate for a more open stitch. This is the stitch which is used on the wrong side of sheer material for shadow embroidery, in which case it is worked closely.

The *German knot* is a pretty form of outlining and should be done with a coarse thread for best results. Worked closely with heavy thread it fairly simulates fancy braiding. It is made from left to right with the needle always pointed towards the worker. Bring the thread up on the stamped line, take a short tight stitch at right angles to and under the stamped line, put the needle under the first loop, drawing the thread loosely, then holding the thread down with the left thumb, make a loose buttonhole-stitch under the same loop to the right of the last stitch. Repeat at regular intervals with the knots close together or separated, according to the effect desired.

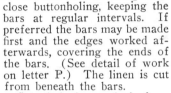

Feather-stitch is a form of loose buttonholing made towards the worker by taking short slant-

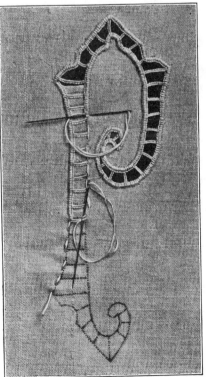

FIG. 14
ITALIAN
CUT-WORK OR
LADDER
STITCH

ing stitches alternately on the left and right of a single stamped line. This stitch is used interchangeably with the herringbone-stitch. There are many variations of this stitch and it can be elaborated by grouping the stitches on each side in clusters of two or three or by varying the length of the stitches.

The cut-work letter partly worked on this page shows the adaptation of the buttonholed bars and buttonholed edges. In this instance the bars are worked first and the edges afterwards instead of as illustrated in Fig. 14. Either method is good and the one to be followed rests entirely with the worker. This letter is an excellent style to use on fine table linen, if a showy letter is desired, but it should not be made much less than four inches high, for if it is made smaller it is not so effective nor so easy to embroider. The spaces between the bars must be wide enough to allow the buttonholing to be done with ease.

FIG. 15. CAT STITCH

In buttonholing the edges of the linen which is to be cut, one row of padding-stitches is all that is necessary and the buttonhole-stitches cannot be too firmly and evenly laid. Be very careful to exactly strike the stamped line in putting in the stitches, for an uneven, broken line of buttonholing completely spoils an embroidered piece.

FIG. 16. GERMAN KNOT

One particular point is the fastening off of one thread and starting another on a buttonholed edge. The thread should be fastened off by sending the needle down on the purl edge over the last stitch on the exact point where it would come up if there had been thread enough to make another stitch. This thread is then fastened on the wrong side by running the needle under the finished stitching. The new thread is fastened on the wrong side and brought up on the inner side of the last purl loop where it would have come up if there had been enough thread to continue the work. Unless the needle is brought up in this way within the tie of the stitch, the break in the edge will be evident.

FIG. 17
FEATHER STITCH

Never cut out the buttonholing until the entire piece is finished, as the work has to be handled so much that the edge is apt to fray. The P on this page is shown with the linen partially cut away, for the sake of illustration.

INITIALS

Materials to Use in Marking

As to the material to use for marking linen, a mercerized cotton embroidery thread is best for embroidering white linen, cotton, or damask. It beats together and gives a smoother appearance than linen thread, and is also easier to handle. The same working cotton which is used for the covering should also form the underlay.

No. 115. Block Letter. Sizes, ⅞, 2, 3, and 4 Inches

Of course the size and quality of thread to be used is governed by the material upon which the work is to be done, and by the style of marking to some extent. A smooth fine linen and a fine dainty design require a fine thread and needle, while a heavy background and bold initials call for coarser thread. If fancy feather-stitching is introduced, a twisted thread is best; perfect eyelets can be made only with fine thread.

Professional monogram workers always use hoops or frames, as very much better embroidery can be done in this manner than by working in the hand, and yet, if one is not accustomed to using hoops, fairly good work may be done without them. Instead of hoops, another method is to baste the linen carefully to a firm foundation such as stiff paper or oilcloth. With care, all

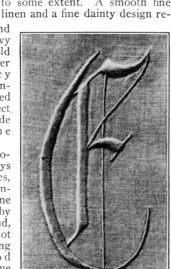

No. 108½. Long and Narrow Old English Initial, Suitable for all Household Linen. Sizes, 1, 1½, 2, 3, 4, 5, and 6 Inches

threads can be fastened on the right side without turning the work. To fasten the thread after working a leaf or stem, run the needle through from one side to the other and back again, and cut the thread close.

White is and always will be considered better than colors for marking linens, not only because it seems more dainty and appropriate,

No. 114 Japanese Initial Sizes, 1, 1½, 2, 2½, 3, and 4 Inches

but because it is far more satisfactory when it comes to the question of laundry, and one may always feel that when her linen is marked in white it is in good taste. This is not saying that colors should never be used

for marking, for frequently a bit of color is introduced into certain styles of lettering with excellent results.

For table linen not designed for every-day service, the initials or monogram may be of the same shade as the principal color employed in the decorative scheme of the room. Some housekeepers mark the towels for each chamber to correspond with the color scheme of the apartment.

No. 09-11-4 Size, 1 Inch Including Spray

Young girls often mark their lingerie with dainty colored initials, selecting always the shade most used for all their personal belongings. Colored initials are also occasionally used on men's handkerchiefs and shirts, and on the pockets or sleeves of girls' middy blouses and smocks.

No. 10-6-4. Script Letter with Leaf Spray, for Outline, Seed Stitch and Satin Embroidery. Size, 1¼ Inches.

Padding

In working initials and monograms on linen, even when the simplest stitches are employed, the greatest care should be exercised in having each line and stitch as nearly perfect as possible, for unless the marking is nicely done it had much better be left off entirely. Nowhere will poor workmanship show more quickly than in marking linen, but the work is not, in the true sense of the word, difficult since all that is needed is the fundamental principles and infinite care.

No. 10-6-2. Fancy Script Sizes, 1½, 2, 3, and 4 Inches

The best needleworkers agree that the most important point in the successful working of initials and monograms is the underlay or padding. After the design is stamped very carefully with sharp, true

ABCDEFGHIJKLM
NOPQRSTUVWXYZ

No. 13-9-71. Line Alphabet. Sizes, 1½, 2, 3, and 4 Inches. Especially Nice Letters for Enclosing in Wreaths. They are so Straight and Simple that They Work up Easily

outlines, taking especial care with small letters, begin by running around them just inside the lines, taking up tiny stitches, and draw to lay flat. Pad by rows of close stem-stitching or outlining, running lengthwise of the design and taking up as little of the material as possible on the wrong side. Fill the space entirely and crowd the rows closely if a high effect is wanted. This part of the work must be firm and compact, but the stitches must not be drawn so tightly as to pull the linen and give the finished product a shrunken appearance.

No. 10-6-6. Block Letter with Forget-me-not. Size, 1⅛ Inches

There is a happy medium to be maintained in the padding. It should be of such a height as to give good relief and be lifted above the surface of the linen, but it should also rise out of and seem a part of the linen and not produce the feeling of its having been placed on the linen.

Padding may be quite high in the centre of the broader section of the letter, but care must be taken to keep it well within the lines of the design with the feeling that the letter is being modeled. Too much emphasis cannot be laid on the importance of this foundation of padding, which will make or mar the finished work.

For very high letters, lay the stitches through the centre of the space to be filled, and after the centre is well covered, take stitches across this work from side to side at a very acute angle, thus binding in the straight stitches. Then before beginning to overlay, place a few more stitches with the direction of the outlines. This is comparatively easy on straight lines; when the curves and little "socks" occur in the design, more careful work within the outlining is necessary.

No. 10-6-3. Rococo Initial Size, 1¾ Inches

Care must be taken that there is no padding under letters where they cross, and never let a slender stem or tendril cross a heavily padded line.

Covering

With a good firm underlay, the covering is not at all difficult, and with reasonable care should be satisfactory. The overlaying should always be placed at right angles to the direction of the lines; this will at once give one the clue to the direction of stitches on all turns and curves. The stitches must be perfectly true and regular and of equal tension, close enough together to form a

smooth surface, but not crowded and overlapping.

In turning a curve it is necessary to crowd the stitches slightly on the inner curve so as to keep them at right angles to the outlines. Before covering the letter, study it carefully, noting the crossings of the letter and the directions of the curves. Work from right to left and on a curve the linen should be held so that the inner edge of the curve will be from the worker.

All super-imposed parts, flowers, balls, bars, crescents, etc., are worked first and a new start made for the letter or monogram proper.

When a monogram is finished it is a good plan to polish it with an ivory stiletto, thus helping to unite the threads and making the work appear very fine and close. The

No. 09-11-9. Size, 2 Inches. Measurement Includes the Spray

proof of a good monogram is in the washing. If the padding is good and the overlay is true and firm, monograms will far outwear the fabric upon which they are worked.

The initials shown on these two pages are suitable for various and sundry purposes, as may be judged by the varying sizes and styles. The small simple letters are nice for handkerchiefs, small napkins, and baby things, the medium sizes for towels, pillow-cases, tea-cloths, and scarfs, and the large sizes for lunch-cloths and sheets.

No. 118. Old English Eyelet Letter for Household Linens. Sizes, 2¾ and 4 Inches

Choosing Styles of Marking

Initials and monograms have more and more become essential for giving distinctiveness to household and personal linen; especially is this remarked in regard to table linen, so it merits the careful attention of all needle-women.

In marking linen, our first consideration is the selection of the styles of letters appropriate to the particular piece of linen to be embroidered. For the dining-room we usually choose rather simple monograms, but when the monogram is the only ornament, it may be as elaborate as one pleases. In the bedroom the marking can be quite fancy, and on women's personal articles the lettering is governed entirely by the taste of the owner, but for men's belong-

No. 101. Sizes, 1, 1½, 2, 3, and 4 Inches. A Style of Script which is Very Easy to Embroider

ings we are more conservative and severe in our taste and choose the most sedate and conventional styles.

We have the opportunity when marking household linens to combine utility and beauty, which is the real basis of decorative art. The idea of identifying is of course first and foremost in the matter of embroidering initialing, but at the same time we can make this very utilitarian idea over into a decorative one by a little careful designing and some good embroidery.

A single elaborate initial or a fancy monogram may be used on the sheet, and the same marking in a smaller size should occupy the pillow-case or bolster-roll.

No. 119. Size, 4⅞ Inches. Measurement Includes the Tendrils. A Style which is Suitable for Shams and Sheets

As for the more personal articles which decorate the dressing-table, one can hardly have the initial too elaborate for the dresser-sets, cushions and handkerchief-cases of fine linen or batiste.

No. 10-6-8. Size, 2 Inches. When Worked as Illustrated this Letter is Very Ornamental

Monograms which are difficult to decipher are not always desirable, although a little mysteriousness is perhaps somewhat attractive. For simple linens, however, a clear, straightforward lettering is in good taste. Letters linked together or grouped are not exactly monograms, but they are a little more easy to manage than the overlapping arrangement which is more truly a monogram, and they are certainly more legible.

Script, block, and Old English lettering are always good, but it is not necessary, because we use these styles, that they should be the same old story all the time. There are many pretty ways of modifying all these letters. If the embroiderer has several good

No. 122. For Table Cloths, Sideboard. and Bureau Scarfs and Centrepieces. Size, 3 Inches

alphabets it will be easy for her to make her own designs by interlacing or grouping various letters in monogram effects. The Old English lettering is not adaptable for interlaced monograms, but can be nicely grouped to form pleasing spots of marking.

No. 103
Sizes ⅜, 1, 1½, 2, 3, and 4 Inches

Japanese letters, quaint with their suggestion of the Orient, are very easily worked as there are few curves and no fanciful scrolls connected with them, and are particularly appropriate when a plain simple marking is desired. They are in fact almost severe in their simplicity, their beauty depending upon their graceful, well-proportioned lines and upon perfect work.

There are two points to be observed in using single initials. They are larger than when two or more are used, and as a rule are more ornate.

The initials on this and the following page are as a whole rather elaborate in style and are sufficiently ornamental to be used alone without any further decoration on the linen.

The small H and A are suitable for handkerchiefs and other small articles, the P and L are good for towels, pillow-cases, bureau-sets, large napkins, and centrepieces, and the three large letters, T, H, and B, are nice on sheets, luncheon-cloths, and large centrepieces.

The letter R at the top of page 9 is popular in large sizes when an ornamental letter which is easy to embroider is desired.

The outlines are in satin-stitch, the dots between the

No. 100. Sizes, ⅜ and 1 Inch. A Dainty Style for Handkerchiefs and Lingerie

lines may be either solid or made into eyelets as illustrated and the tendrils are in feather-stitch. On the larger letters the fancy stitching may be more elaborate, more feathery and frond like. This is a satisfactory style for large towels, sheets and shams.

The Placing of Initials and Monograms

Questions constantly arise as to the proper positions of monograms on linen. The fact is, the monogram or initial, as the case may be, should be placed conveniently, and it is in reality a matter of common sense and good taste; however, it is very easy to reduce common sense to rules, and perhaps wise to do so. There is no definite rule and Fashion allows much latitude for individual preference.

On a table-cloth, the monogram should preferably be about two inches from the edge of the table, at the left of the hostess, if only one monogram is used.

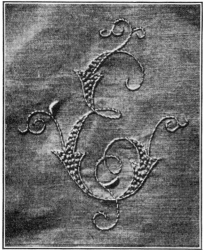

No. 106. Sizes, 1, 1½, 2, 3, and 4 Inches. An Attractive Letter which is Easy to Embroider

When two sets are used, as is often the case, they are differently arranged; the most effective position being on each side of the centre, so placed as to be at a proper distance from both centrepiece and plates.

The foregoing rules apply to plain linen cloths where there is no embroidery design to consider. When one is puzzled to know where to place the marking on an embroidered luncheon-cloth, she should be guided by the design, placing the monogram or initial in plain view and in some space which seems suitable. If it is possible to put it on a diagonal line from the centre to the left of the hostess, then it stands the best chance of not being covered with some plate or platter.

Napkins are usually marked in the diagonal of one corner with the base of the letter towards the

No. 10-6-9. Shown Full Size, 2¼ Inches, which Includes the Daisy

corner. The rule for so placing the marking on a medium size napkin is to fold it in halves, and then in halves again, forming a square; fold the square on both diagonals and crease. Just where the

No. 09-10-49. Sizes, 3 and 5 Inches. Initial in Feather-Stitch, Outline and Eyelets

creased lines cross, put the monogram. Where there is a satin stripe above the hem, the initials are put on the stripe. Often it seems advisable to have the marking quite near the corner.

Sometimes the letters are put in the corner of the napkin with the base turned towards the right side, keeping the letters square with the grain of the linen.

Very handsome napkins are sometimes marked in the middle of the third of one side, that is, the napkin is folded in thirds one way, then in thirds again, and the monogram placed in the centre of the square thus formed, not in the corner, but in the side of the napkin. Occasionally very large napkins are marked in the very centre with the letters running parallel with the thread of the linen.

On fancy tea and luncheon napkins the initial alone is often used inside a wreath or in conjunction with a spray or ornamental motif, and usually the design occupies a space quite near the corner.

Centrepieces and doilies are not often marked un-

No. 113. Size, 4 Inches. A Beautiful Letter for Table Cloths and Scarfs

No. 130. SCRIPT LETTER WITH FORGET-ME-NOT SPRAY. FULL SIZE, 1½ INCHES, INCLUDING SPRAY

less they are almost entirely free of other ornamentation, in which case the letter or monogram is placed about an inch from the scallop or hem.

Oblong end pieces and carving cloths are marked in the middle of one side or in the left corner with the base of the letters towards the longer side.

There are also some general rules governing the marking of bedroom

No. 10-6-7. FANCY BLOCK LETTER. SIZES, 2¼, 3, AND 4 INCHES. NUMERALS SAME STYLE IN 3-INCH SIZE

linen. Sheets should have the letters in the middle of the top about an inch from the hem or two inches from the scallop, if scallops are used. The base of the letters should be turned towards the hem or scallop so that when the sheet is put on the bed face down and the end turned back over the spread with the fold just touching the bolster, the letters will be easily read. The exact placing of the monogram depends somewhat upon its size and also the depth of the sheet which is turned over as well as upon whatever other design is used. Only the top sheet is embroidered, the bottom one being finished with a plain hem.

Pillow-cases have the letters placed just above the hems in the middle of the top side with the base towards the hem or scallop. In the case of a square pillow, ruffled or lace trimmed, the monogram may be placed in the upper left corner.

Bolster-cases have the marking either at one end like the pillow-case or on top in the centre if a large enough initial or monogram is used.

If shams and pillow-scarfs are marked they usually

No. 107. PLAIN SCRIPT. SIZES, ⅜, ⅝, 1, 1½, 2, 2½, 3, 4, 5, AND 6 INCHES

No. 107. SIZES, ⅜, ⅝, 1, 1½, 2, 2½, 3, 4, 5, AND 6 INCHES. A SIMPLE AND PLEASING LETTER FOR HOUSEHOLD LINENS

have a large elaborate initial or monogram in the centre, which may or may not contain some other ornamentation.

Bureau-scarfs are often marked in the middle of the front edge within some space especially designed for

No. 131. SCRIPT LETTER WITH ROSEBUDS. SIZES, 1¼ AND 2 INCHES

the monogram, or they are marked on the end if the scarf hangs over. The pincushion should contain the same style of lettering in smaller size placed in the centre of the top cover.

Personal wear is marked to a limited extent and inconspicuously. The upper undergarments have small lettering placed at the middle or left of the front as the embroidery design admits, and drawers and petticoats are marked on the ruffles at the left side.

Handkerchiefs for both men and women are marked in the corner, after the manner of napkins with the difference that the letters are near the corner and they are simpler in design. If a spray is used on handkerchief, it is usually placed just above the initial.

Monograms or single initials are sometimes used on men's shirts, and are placed on the left sleeve half way between the elbow and the cuff. These are usually quite conventional in design, and about an inch or an inch and a half high. A slender narrow letter may be taller than a blocky one. Night shirts and pajamas are marked on the pockets.

On the dainty little accessories of the toilet, such as glove and handkerchief cases, veil, ribbon, and card-cases, the marking may be placed in any arrangement which seems best to suit the shape and style of the article, usually in the centre of the front, but when the front is covered entirely with the design, it is placed on the back in a wreath or scroll.

The initials on this page are all in the script style except the block B in the centre. All of these are practical, useful letters which are not especially difficult to work, and yet are quite ornamental for simple bedroom or dining-room linen. If a more decorative effect is desired, two or three initials may be used together in a line instead of a

No. 09-11-5. FANCY SCRIPT IN SATIN AND SEED STITCH
SIZE, 2 INCHES

monogram. This suggestion applies to all the letters on the page except the C, which seems quite complete in itself with its little spray of blossoms underneath.

Sizes

In selecting the size of an initial or monogram to be embroidered, there are a number of factors to be carefully considered. First we must know the size and shape of the space which is to contain the marking, give consideration to the weave of the material, and choose the style of letter, and the *shape* of the letter or monogram will determine to a great extent the proper height for any particular purpose. A much taller thin letter can be used on an article than a wide blocky letter; a taller diamond-shaped monogram can be used than a square or wide one, so we really have to consider the number of square inches occupied as well as the height, although the consideration may be subconscious or intuitive.

Still there are some general rules for sizes which any wise needleworker will heed in her marking and they are as follows: Table-cloths, 3 to 8 inches; napkins, 1 to 3 inches; guest towels, 1 to 3 inches; large towels, 2 to 4 inches; bedspread, 6 to 14 inches; sheets, 2 to 6 inches; pillow-cases, 2 to 4 inches; handkerchiefs, ¼ to 1 inch; lingerie, 1 to 2 inches.

It is readily understood that a two-inch monogram which spreads out from side to side covering a space in width of three inches or more is really larger than a single narrow two-inch letter or a round or diamond-shaped two-inch monogram, hence the choice of sizes for the same articles in the foregoing suggestions.

Some housekeepers prefer a very small letter or monogram enclosed in some simple design such as a wreath of flowers or embroidered leaves.

One very important point

No. 09-11-7. SIZE OF WREATH, 1¼ x 1½ INCHES; LETTER, ⅝-INCH. FOR HANDKERCHIEFS, LINGERIE, AND BABY THINGS

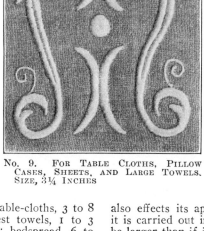

No. 9. FOR TABLE CLOTHS, PILLOW CASES, SHEETS, AND LARGE TOWELS. SIZE, 3¼ INCHES

to consider in selecting a certain size and style of letter is whether the particular style chosen will work up nicely in the certain size desired, for there are many letters and monograms which are perfectly satisfactory only within a limited range of sizes; if they are enlarged too much they look barren, and if they are reduced too much they seem crowded and are too complicated to work easily, therefore we should consider the different styles in relation to size.

No. 132. SCALLOPED LETTER
SIZES, 1½, 3, AND 5 INCHES

The letters and monograms with cut-work are not practical, or rather they are difficult to work, if made small, they should therefore be chosen only when they can be made fairly large. It is obvious that this is so if one is acquainted with the principles of cut-work.

Here it may be well to mention that initials and monograms are measured in height and that the given measurement includes the extremes of the ornamentation accompanying the lettering unless otherwise stated, and this fact must also be considered when choosing a monogram. If there are tendrils or leaves extending above and below which have to be counted into the measurement, then the lettering proper of course does not appear so large, and it would not be so large, as it would if the letters themselves extended to the limits of the dimensions.

The method of working a letter also effects its apparent size to a certain extent. If it is carried out in solid embroidery, it will appear to be larger than if it is worked in outline or some loose open stitchery such as feather-stitch.

No. 108. REGULATION OLD ENGLISH LETTER. SIZES, ⅜, ½, ⅝, 1, 1½, 2, 3, 4, AND 5 INCHES

No. 15-4-2. Sizes, 1, 1½, and 2 Inches. The Above Arrangement Shows Three Letters on a Towel

No. 129. Medallion and Letter. Size of Medallion, 3 Inches; of Letter, 1¼ Inches.

Generally speaking, the rules for lettering on linen are more arbitrary than those demanded by French embroidery, of which it is an important branch, but nevertheless they are not iron bound, and each worker can exercise her artistic sense and give individuality by her selection of designs, placing and methods of working. It is perfectly safe to embroider white linens in white and in French and eyelet designs. One might almost say in any French and eyelet design, for it is hard for designers to go far astray and make a hopelessly bad design in that particular style.

No. 128. Letter with Leaf Spray. Size, 1-Inch.

The small initials and name on this page are in just the right style for lingerie, personal toilet articles, bags, cases and baby things. The floral touches lend the proper ornamentation to the letters, and in the case of the name "Elisabeth," the spray not only serves to combine the lettering, but makes of the marking a decorative ornament which is sufficient in itself. All the work in the name is in fine satin-stitch except the tiny eyelet at the centre of the flower.

Where a striking, bold design is required, No. 09-11-8 is a good model. Something like Richelieu embroidery,

it differs in a very material point, for its outlines are corded instead of being buttonholed. The outlines of the letter are run very closely and evenly, then threads are carried across for the bars which are wrapped firmly and afterwards the edges of the letters are worked closely in a fine over and over satin-stitch which must be so firm that the linen can be cut away next to it without fear of any fraying. It serves instead of buttonholing.

The three letters D H D, No. 15-4-2, while not a monogram, serve in the place of one, and are of a style which is very easy to embroider. It is a good plan for the amateur to begin with straight lines similar to these, as shaded lines, that is, lines which are wider in some parts than others, are much more difficult to keep symmetrical.

No. 10-6-1. Shown Full Size, 1⅛ inches

The letter P in the medallion forms a nice spot for the corner of a small lunch-cloth, and it is also good for pillow-slips and fine towels. This design is entirely in satin-stitch except the calyxes and some of the flower petals, which are outlined and filled with seed-stitches.

The two small letters, E and A, are suitable for napkins, lingerie, bags, cases and pincushions, and may be used alone or in connection with whatever other embroidery ornaments the article, as the little sprays and flowerets are of such a simple inconspicuous character that they will easily harmonize with almost any style of decoration.

In working these small letters on sheer fabrics it is necessary to use very fine thread and a fine needle to obtain best results.

No. 09-11-8. Letter with Cut-Work Background. Size, 4 Inches

No. 09-11-6. Full Size. Any Name May Be Made with the Fancy Spray

MONOGRAMS

THEIR USES AND ADAPTATIONS

No. 157. (E J M) In Circular Effect, and Very Easy to Embroider

No. 158. (L P N) A Square Composed of Old English Letters

THE suggestions on the preceding pages as to the selection of styles, sizes, placing and methods of embroidering, apply equally to monograms and initials, for whether one or the other is used is a matter of space or personal preference, for the marking of household linens is a matter of taste.

At one moment we see a monogram on every possible occasion and again it is a single letter; at other times no embroidered letters are to be seen. At present all linen must be marked in some way, either with an inconspicuous marking or with an elaborate ornamental monogram which forms the principal decoration on the article.

At any time if one likes to have the linen marked, there is not the slightest reason why one should not, always providing that the embroidery is well done and that the design is in good taste. Such marking makes linens more valuable, more personal, and more interesting to the present generation and, as many of us know from personal experience, intensely interesting and valuable to those who are fortunate enough to inherit them in good condition.

On these pages one has a great variety of styles to choose from, all practical for embroidery, some more suitable for one purpose than another, but all in good taste.

The design above which shows the let-

ters fitted together to form an almost perfect circle makes a very pleasing semblance of a monogram and yet the letters are not interlaced in any way, but each fits into its own particular part of the circle. In effect the same can be said of the Old English letters forming a square on the diagonal. It is obvious that these letters are entirely unsuited for interlacing, and yet when arranged as shown here they form a charming combination. Both of these styles are suitable to use on all household linens and will work up well in any reasonable size.

The dainty spray with its quaint monogram at the bottom of the page is quite ornamental enough to be used alone on a baby's sheet and pillow or on a carriage pillow. Enlarged to about nine inches wide and six deep it makes a pretty decoration for a bolster roll or sham. Three letters can be used equally as well as two in this design and would in most cases make a more pleasing combination.

The ribbon effect in ladder-stitch or Italian cut-work is particularly attractive and adds an open lightness to the design which is more satisfactory than the ribbon would be if worked solid. This stitch is not difficult to master and there are details of it in the first part of the book making it very clear to any one without experience wishing to attempt it for the first time.

No. 09-11-10. Monogram, 1½ Inches. No. 09-11-11. Wreath, 3 x 4½ Inches. The Monogram May Contain Two or Three Letters

ALL the monograms shown on these two pages are graceful and practical and are suitable for either dining-room or chamber linen. They are not extreme in style of design or stitchery, and therefore may be quite easily made in different sizes to suit different requirements so as to have an entire set of linen in the same design.

It would be hard to find a more pleasing, well balanced design than that shown in No. 09-11-12. Its slender lines are prevented by the spray which forms the background from giving a spindling effect and it also helps to hold the letters together as one unit of decoration. In working these letters it is necessary for perfect results to take great care in keeping the sides of the letters parallel and keeping the lines regular and straight.

The graceful monogram No. 111 shows the dif-

No. 09-11-12. Two Letters with Spray in Monogram Effect. The Letters Themselves are 2 Inches High

ferent steps to be taken in working a simple monogram. As has been stated before under the subject of padding, too much stress cannot be laid upon the importance of having a firm foundation made before attempting to cover the letter, for success or failure depends upon it. The letters must be clearly stamped or carefully drawn, as one cannot get good results

No. 117. (M A B) Practical in all Sizes for Household Linens

if the lines are not sharp and clear, as they are to be accurately followed.

With a fine needle and thread go over the outlines, taking tiny running-stitches, being careful to preserve the relative positions of the letters where they cross each other. This preliminary work is simply to regulate the line as a guide to the needle, many workers dispensing with it entirely.

The first row of padding, which consists of stem or outline stitch, is put very close to the running thread, as shown in the illustration between the two bars on "B". After following the running line

No. 14-1-13. The Letter of the Last Name is made Large and Important

around the entire letter, continue to put rows of stem stitches close together, slightly lapping those towards the centre until the whole is neatly padded.

The upper curve of the "G" shows it ready for the covering thread. In covering, work first the bars, balls, or any superimposed parts, and then work the main parts of the letters. Insert the needle just under the running thread, but never a thread beyond in coming out on the other edge. Work from right to left, keeping the needle at right angles to the letter and crowding the stitches on the inner, and spreading them slightly on the outer edge when necessary.

In working the "G", commence at the crescent, cover closely to the dividing line, bring the needle up between the lines of separation and bar, under which slip the needle and work up to the dividing line, then proceed as before. On the upper part of the "G" commence at the points of the little leafy parts, and work to the end. In so working the curves are easily managed. Next work the horns of the "G," commencing

at the tip of the lower and the dividing line of the upper.

The eyelets in this design are worked in the usual way by running the thread around the stamped line, cutting and shaping the opening into a perfect circle, and then whipping over and over very closely and evenly with short stitches which touch but do not overlap. In fastening the thread after making

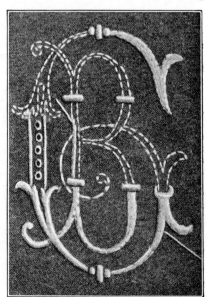

No. 111. (B G) Showing a Monogram in Process of Working

an eyelet, leave the last stitch loose and put the needle down through this stitch to the wrong side, now draw the thread up tightly and take another little stitch on the wrong side before cutting the thread. A very fine needle must be used to work eyelets successfully.

The single lines which appear on each side of the eyelets in the "G" are made in satin outline, which is described and illustrated in the first part of the book among the stitches which are shown in detail.

The monogram No. 117 on page 14 is one of the simplest and most popular designs for general household marking, not only because of its being so easy to embroider, but its simple lines are most pleasing and

No. 123. THE LETTERS ARE 2 INCHES HIGH

No. 13-8-12. (L B W) ESPECIALLY NICE IN JUST THIS SIZE, 2 INCHES, FOR PERSONAL ARTICLES

decorative when nicely worked. This style is satisfactory in almost any size and may be used on all manner of household and personal linen. It will be noticed that the middle letter is slightly different from the others in that it has a pointed bulge on the widest parts.

No. 14-1-13, F R F, is an attractive, practical monogram for table linen and also for men's articles, as it is very conventional in design and in stitchery, and is entirely legible and easy to embroider. Some care must be taken to keep the little open spaces open and regular in outline, but then every monogram must be worked with care if it is properly worked.

L B W, No. 13-8-12, is perhaps one of the simplest and least conventional monograms shown, in fact it may almost be called careless, and yet it is very pleasing in de-

sign and any needleworker would realize at a glance that it is particularly easy to embroider. The lines of the letters run from wide to narrow in such an easy gradation that it is not difficult to follow them. All that is necessary is to have the padding firm and regular and keep the covering stitches the same.

In No. 123 one will notice a striking similarity to No. 9-11-12. The designs are practically the same with the exception of the sprays which are slightly different; the letters themselves are the same.

The leaves of the spray which unites the letters are outlined and then filled with seed-stitches, fine little back-stitches made at regular intervals and quite closely filling the spaces. This same stitch, made even more regularly and closely, is used in the "F" in the monogram No. 15-4-3, while the other two letters are in voided satin-stitch. Very often in monogram work the middle letter is made in a different stitch, and this not only helps to make the monogram more legible, but adds to the beauty of the design and lends variety to the work.

This design is very nice on table linen, especially if a rather large monogram is desired, and it is also good in small sizes, as it is simple in line and quite easy to embroider. However, if it is made very small, it will be difficult to carry out the seed-stitch effect in the middle letter and this will have to be worked solid, also in a small size the side letters would be more practical in a single padded line.

No. 15-4-3. (S H F) GOOD IN 4-INCH SIZE FOR LUNCHEON CLOTH

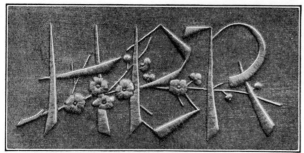

No. 13-3-48. (H B R) JAPANESE MONOGRAM

S OME very exacting housekeepers like to have all the linen in the dining-room marked to correspond with the table linen, a fad not irksome to the woman who wisely selects a particular style of monogram and letter for all her household linen, thereby making it personal and distinctive, a result always so much desired. Monotony of a design often repeated is avoided by the method of working, by using sometimes the monogram and sometimes the initials, and by the employment of shields, scrolls, and sprays as a background as well as by varying the stitchery.

The fastidious hostess who wishes to give charm and individuality to her linen will use care and circumspection in her selection of marking, and it is seldom in such a home is the fanciful and ornate seen in the dining-room.

In monogram work the Gothic is always charming and in good taste, and the letters may be worked out simply or very elaborately. A lovely example of Gothic letters is the monogram M I A, No. 14-1-12, which is exceedingly clear. This little group of letters is decorative and yet it is not complicated or overornate. Other good examples of simple clear-cut letters are the groups H P C and L A. Either of these is easy to work, but the very easiest letters are those with straight lines which can be made to coincide with the grain of the material. When one once gets started making a straight line into the thread of the fabric it is difficult to go astray.

The lovely little spray and buttonhole, No. 12-3-35. is a reminder of the days when men's shirt fronts were embroidered. These same sprays are being re-

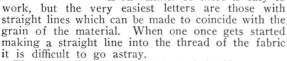

No. 12-3-35. SPRAY AND BUTTONHOLE. SIZE, 2¼ INCHES

No. 15-2-12. (E W N) FOR TABLE CLOTHS AND SHEETS

No. 14-1-9. (H P C) GOOD IN 3-INCH SIZE

vived now for ornamenting the otherwise homely buttonholes of shirt-waists and for the flaps of bags and cases. A fine design of this nature must be beautifully worked to be at all effective and satisfactory, and this can be done only with a very fine needle and thread, but any one can learn to do it with patience and practice.

The Japanese letters with the spray of cherry blossoms through them may be used effectively in the centre of a serving-tray or on the corner of a luncheon-cloth. The stiffness of the plain letters is relieved by the introduction of the spray, and the spray and letters together make a charming combination. These letters are three inches tall, and with this arrangement the effect is that of a much larger monogram than the circle No. 14-1-9, which also measures three inches.

As has been stated before, the arrangement of the letters must always be taken into consideration when the size of a monogram is being decided upon.

The monograms E W N, A E A, and A T B are all quite elaborate and ornamental and they are also

No. 14-1-18. (A E A) SUITABLE FOR BUREAU COVERS, SHEETS, AND LUNCH CLOTHS IN 5-INCH SIZE

No. 14-1-12. (M I A) THIS IN FIVE SIZES IS GOOD FOR MARKING HOUSEHOLD LINENS

in good design and are very pleasing. They may be used alone on any piece of household linen, and will be ornament enough in themselves. The same may be said of M L L, No. 14-1-14, which, while not embellished with sprays of flowers, is composed of ornamental letters in a pleasing arrangement.

The designs shown on this page are suitable for various purposes as may suit the fancy of the worker. The monogram C N C, No. 15-4-1, is of a graceful, simple style which is particularly suitable for towels and pillow-cases; it is also nice for large napkins, and can easily be

No. 14-1-17. (A T B) Enlarged this is Beautiful for Bedspreads

made larger for table-cloths, scarfs, and tea-cloths. This is a design which is both easy to embroider and easy to read when it is embroidered.

The monogram H J, No. 16-1-2, designed for a set of embroidered spreads for twin beds, is very graceful in its tall, slender effect. It should be about fourteen inches tall for this purpose, and being so slender, it does not look large in this height. A six-inch size in the same design is suitable for pillow-cases, and the style is such that it can be reduced still more without losing its character or

No. 14-1-14. (M L L) An Elaborate Monogram which is Worked in Satin Outline, Seed-Stitch, and Satin Dots

becoming commonplace. The letters are worked entirely in satin-stitch except for the triangular spaces which are filled with seed-stitches.

This monogram is a pretty style for three letters as well as for two, but naturally the arrangement would be somewhat different from the combination here shown, as each monogram has to be planned individually to suit the best arrangement of the letters employed.

The housekeeper will find that when it comes to having dozens of articles marked, it will sensibly deplete even a well-filled pocketbook, unless she is

No. 15-4-1. (C N C) A Good Script Monogram for a Towel

willing and competent to do the work herself, and this book is written with the express purpose of helping her over the difficulties that await her, and making the work as easy and fascinating as possible, for marking linen is a very fascinating branch of embroidery,—an art in itself.

It is not necessary that the amateur begin with the simplest style of letters, for often the monograms which are composed of the plain lines and simple curves require the greatest care in the working, since their beauty consists in their entire perfection, while if some fancy stitchery were introduced or a garland of flowers combined with the letters, there would be a chance of bringing out some other attractive points than the absolute excellence of satin-stitch, which would naturally be the stitch employed for unadorned letters.

Care must be exercised in choosing the proper monogram for the particular linen to be embroidered, and the proper stitches for the monogram, then with suitable needles and cotton, and a fair knowledge of embroidery in general, the work should be satisfactory.

No. 16-1-2. (H J) Being Long and Narrow, this will Fit Nicely on a Bedspread Strip. Three Letters can be Used

WHERE there are little inserts in the design of a monogram such as the triangular spaces in the S H F, No. 14-1-10, very great care must be taken to keep the outline. It is so easy to encroach upon the open space within the lines of the triangles, but this must not be done, for the beauty of such a design is

No. 14-1-10. (S H F) A Good Style for Table Linen

dependent upon a very clear-cut outline. Of course the stamping must be true, and if it is not, the outlines should be corrected with a pencil before embroidering.

A graceful medallion for the centre of a bed-spread is given in No. 15-4-5. This wreath may contain either a two or three letter monogram, and when the letters are large, as in this case, it is a good idea to divide the lines and work them in the

No. 15-4-5. A Very Graceful Medallion for the Centre of a Bedspread. The Monogram is just half the Height of the Wreath

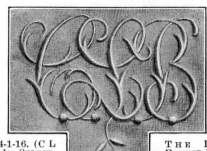

No. 14-1-16. (C L B) In Select-ing a Size, the Spray Must Be Con-sidered in the Measurement.

The Drop Flower Helps this Design to Fit Nicely into a Corner of a Square Cloth

No. 15-4-7. (L H J) With Satin Outline and Fancy Seed Stitching; Good in 8 and 10 Inch Sizes

voided satin-stitch. When they grow narrow they can merge into the single line. The flowers and leaves are all in padded satin-stitch and the flower centres are eyelets.

In No. 14-1-16 the letters C L B are read in their order, as they are of one size and style and are intended to be so read. This is an especially pretty arrangement and is nice to use on pillow-cases, sheets, and towels.

The medallion L H J, No. 15-4-7, is a beautiful example of the true monogram, and the outline it-self of these letters forms the diamond. These let-ters are all outlined in fine satin outline and filled with different seed and diaper stitches, so that while the work is harmonious the letters are easily dis-tinguished one from another.

While the design R W is not, in the true sense

of the word, a monogram, it requires a special arrangement and placing, and is not satisfactory unless the balance is perfect. This design is practical only for two letters, and it is a very nice idea for marking large towels, sheets, and table-cloths.

The B S, No. 15-4-4, is also suitable for the corner of a table-cloth, and it is an arrangement

No. 16-1-3. A Pleasing Arrangement of 3-Inch Letters

which is both very graceful and easy to embroider. This can be used on sheets and pillow-cases, towels and scarfs, and in fact almost any household linen.

E S O, in its simple frame, is as graceful and satisfactory a monogram as one could wish for, and the monogram alone, without its frame, is very pleasing

seeming too heavy, as it possibly would if the entire design were worked in padded satin - stitch. There is one fault which must be guarded against in working this design, and that is not to have the oval which surrounds the lettering too tightly worked, that is, the padding must be put in with firm stitches but not of such a tension as to draw the linen even slightly. There is a tendency with some people to make the stitches so very tight that when the linen is wet it puckers all around the marking and can be pressed smooth only with difficulty, and where a continuous line surrounds the monogram, as in this instance, one is more in danger of making this mistake, but it is a mistake which can easily be avoided if one is careful.

In pressing a monogram after it has been laundered, it should be placed face down on a heavily padded board with a thin cloth over it and pressed quite firmly with a hot iron. Care must be taken not to press the embroidery flat and thus spoil the very effect that has been striven for, but the linen must be smooth.

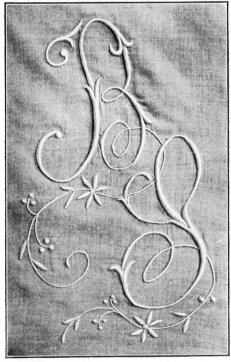

No. 15-4-4. A Graceful Arrangement for Use on Bedroom Linen

and may be used for a variety of purposes. The measurement given is for the entire design, measuring from the extreme top of the bow to the tip of the leaf, and the monogram itself is just about half of this dimension; so this fact must be taken into consideration when choosing a size and allowance made so that the letters will not be too small.

This design is particularly nice ten, twelve, or even fourteen inches high on a bedspread, but it can be worked satisfactorily as small as four inches and may be used on both bedroom and dining-room linens. If it is used with the frame on a luncheon-cloth, the napkins may be marked with the monogram only, made about two inches tall.

The seed-stitch which is used in the ribbon gives a pleasing variety and keeps the embroidery from

No. 15-2-10. (E S O) Suitable for Table and Bed Linen. The Monogram is about Half as High as the Wreath, and is very Pretty when Used Alone

No. 15-2-8. (A M G) Suitable for Handkerchiefs in Small Size, but May Be Enlarged for Other Uses

THERE is no fixed and fast rule for the arrangement of letters in a monogram, for they should be placed so as to make the prettiest possible effect, and naturally some combinations of letters assemble to better advantage than others, but there are several points to consider. If the letters are all of one size, they are arranged in the order that they are to be read, as illustrated in the styles A M G and H G C on this page, but if the letters are to be of different sizes, different designs, or to be worked in different stitches, the letter of the surname should be the most prominent. This idea is plainly illustrated in No. 15-2-11, A J G in which the "G" is conspicuous both because of its size and method of working.

In No. 15-2-6 the letters are read J P H, just as they are arranged, as there is not enough difference in the size of the letters to read them otherwise. This monogram and the one corresponding to it on the opposite page, No. 15-2-4, are both especially suitable for marking men's belongings, as they are simple and conventional in design. They are worked entirely in padded satin-stitch and are quite easy to embroider. The J P H is best between one and four inches, but L G S may be enlarged to almost any size and still be practical and pretty.

The small monograms, A M G and E P O at the tops of the pages are nice for handkerchiefs, napkins, doilies, handkerchief-cases, pincushions and other small articles. The E P O is an exception to the rule of measuring a monogram by its extreme height, as in this case the size of the letters themselves determine the price of the monogram, for there is no reason why these letters, because they are arranged one above the other, should be more expensive than the same size letters arranged side by side.

Nos. 15-2-11 and 15-2-9 in three-inch size fit beautifully on bureau-scarfs, pincushions, handkerchief and glove cases, pillow-slips and towels, and in larger sizes, four and five inches, are suitable for sheets and table-cloths. These designs are quite ornamental and really form

No. 15-2-11. (A J G) Especially Nice on a Lunch Cloth

sufficient decoration in themselves unless one wishes to use scallops on the edges of the linen.

The cut-work design, No. 15-2-5, is made with wrapped instead of buttonholed bars, and the edges of the cut spaces as well as the solid lines are all in over-and-over satin-stitch. If this stitch is carefully padded and carefully covered, it is equally as satisfactory as buttonholing; some workers prefer it to buttonholing since it seems to harmonize better with the solid parts of the design. This style of letter is not practical under three inches if it is to be worked as illustrated. When it is made smaller, it should be worked entirely solid, and even so it makes a very pretty monogram. Worked in open ladder-stitch it is especially attractive on linen sheets and lunch-cloths, and it can be enlarged to eight or ten inches for shams or bolster-rolls.

C A H is an ornamental script monogram which is always in good taste for any household or personal linens. It is perhaps at its best in sizes from three to five inches, but it can easily be made in almost any other size, either smaller or larger, and it will still be practical and easy to work, but in a very small size the little decorative divergencies

No. 15-2-5. (H G C) In Ladder-Stitch with Satin-Stitch Edges and Wrapped Bars

No. 15-2-6. (J P H) For Marking Men's Linen

No. 159. (H B R) Suitable for Table Linen and Articles for Men

No. 15-2-9. (E F E) A Pretty Arrangement Within
a Circle

No. 15-2-7. (E
P O) For
Hand-
kerchiefs

and the effect is much prettier and more pleasing and gives a nice contrast to the regular satin-stitch of the basket and the letters. It will be noticed that the outer leaves on the spray are worked as eyelets. The centres of the flowers are also eyelets and this openwork is especially attractive with the hemstitch effect of the basket handle.

Besides being suitable for pillow-cases, this basket design may be used alone for enclosing a monogram on the corner of a square tea-cloth or on odd pieces of linen. It is also nice for guest-towels and may be worked with a touch of color in the flowers and basket.

When one takes up the subject of embroidering household linens the question becomes a great one, for here individual taste and preference for one form of needlework over another is brought into play, and there are always little fads and fancies in embroidery to be considered; but when it comes to the marking of linen with initials and monograms, the worker may feel fairly safe in clinging to the more conservative styles for those pieces of linen which she expects to last at least a generation. In the matter of towels and wearing apparel which are more or less transient, she may be more frivolous and use the fads of the moment.

should be simplified. This design is very pleasing on bedroom linens, and may with satisfaction be used on all the chamber linens.

A very quaint idea is to have the letters enclosed within an effect of a basket handle, as in No. 15-4-6, which illustrates a section of a pillow-case. The letters themselves are very pretty and one, two or three may be used. As illustrated, the two letters make a graceful combination. The flowers and lines of the design are worked in satin-stitch with some of the leaves solid and some as eyelets, and the unique little handle of the basket is a pretty little open stitch known as "Hemstitching." It is made over a coarse thread with a very large needle and fine thread, the large needle making the holes in the linen and the thread binding them. It is not a difficult stitch, as may be seen from the detail which shows the stitch in progress, but it must be made on fairly sheer fabric. However, if one does not care to use this stitch, a simple outline, cat-stitch, or the German knot stitch will not spoil the design.

The little forget-me-nots in this design are worked in the French style, that is, they are worked from the centre out instead of taking the stitches across the petals,

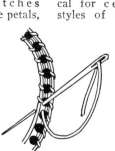

No. 15-2-14. (C A H) May Be Easily Worked in
3 and 4 Inch Sizes

All the designs shown on these pages are sensible, serviceable and practical. Some are more elaborate and ornamental than others, but they are styles of which one will not easily tire, which we can live with and still be pleased with after years of service.

Of course many of the designs admit of different methods of working from those illustrated, and the embroiderer must use her own good taste and discrimination when it comes to the decision of the stitches to be employed. The size of the letters in many instances will have to determine whether or not they are practical for certain styles of stitches.

No. 15-4-6. A Pretty Pillow-Case
Design

Detail of "Hem-
stitching" on
Handle of Basket,
No. 15-4-6

No. 15-2-4. (L G S) Appropriate
for a Man's Shirt Sleeve

21

NO. 16-1-4 is a very pretty, neat arrangement of letters within a decorative design rather than a true monogram, and the placement of the letters must be absolutely true in relation to the sprays and dots, otherwise the effect will be more or less spoiled. It is better to have the letters perforated in the design and the whole stamped at once rather than try to place the letters in after the decorative motifs have been stamped.

In working small dots such as enter into this design, a great deal of care must be taken to keep them as round as possible, and this is no easy matter, as experienced workers will testify. The wisest plan is to put in a few padding stitches extending almost to the stamped lines but not quite touching them, then put on the covering at right angles to the padding. The result will be much more pleasing if the stitches in all the dots run in the same direction.

This design is appropriate for bedroom and dining-room linens, and may also be used on wearing apparel. If a simpler effect is desired, just the three

No. 15-2-13.   (F F R) For Table Linens

In working this design, it is best to work all the supplementary parts, bars, tendrils and balls, before the letters proper are commenced, then these must be padded, taking particular care to go neatly around the little indentures which occur at the tops and sides of the letters. When made in a very large size, these letters would work up well in fancy seed-stitches with the outlines and tendrils only in satin-stitch.

Sometimes there is doubt as to the proper letters to use in marking linen, especially household linen, so perhaps a word of suggestion on that line would not be amiss.

When a girl is marking her bridal linen, she should use her own monogram, or if she is using only one letter on her linens, it should be the initial of her surname. Not until after she is married does she use her husband's name, which is then her own, on her linen; and a married woman uses her own monogram, not her husband's, on all household linens. She uses the initial of her first name, the initial of her middle name and the initial of her own (and husband's) surname.

All bridal presents which are marked should be marked with the bride's maiden initial or monogram.

No. 16-1-4.   (M E A) A Nice Monogram Effect for Household Linens

letters with the inside spray and accompanying dots makes a pleasing little spot.

The word "Baby," No. 10-6-5, is useful for marking a baby's towel, crib sheets, pillow, carriage robe, and bath-mat or lap-pad. The letters themselves are padded quite heavily and covered closely with satin-stitches, but before this is done the flowers and leaves are worked. The leaves are in voided satin-stitch and the forget-me-nots are worked without padding with the stitches running from the centre towards the tips of the petals. This stitch makes a charming little flower and lends variety to the work. It is no harder to work than the ordinary satin-stitch taken across the petals; in fact, some people find it much simpler to do. The centres of the tiny flowers are eyelets made in the usual way.

The monogram F F R on this page is good in any size from one inch up, but of course the design must necessarily be somewhat modified in the varying sizes. In a four-inch size it is suitable for a luncheon or table cloth, and if one wishes napkins to match, the small ones should be marked with a one-inch monogram and the larger size with two-inch letters.

No. 10-6-5.   For the Baby's Carriage Robe, Blanket, or Pillow

MONOGRAMMED LINENS

THE SELECTION OF LINEN

EVERY housekeeper delights in a goodly supply of household linen, and it is a pretty custom for a girl at her marriage to have a linen chest filled that will serve the purposes of her household for years to come. These pieces should, of course, be for both bedroom and dining-room, and it is true economy to buy an adequate supply of linen at one time, for by this method every article will last much longer than if a few changes are made to do duty constantly.

An ordinary outfit that will give good satisfaction is one dozen table-cloths, six dozen napkins, six or seven dozen towels, one dozen pairs of sheets, two dozen pillow-slips, several tea-cloths, and sufficient centrepieces, sideboard-covers, scarfs, doilies, tray-cloths, and bureau and stand covers to give sufficient change when some articles are in the laundry.

In selecting table linen, individual judgment dictates the quality and number for different occasions. A dozen table-cloths might be divided as follows: Two damask as handsome as the purse allows, four less admirable for less formal occasions, and six for every-day use, strong and of close weave. These of course will be supplemented with lunch-cloths, breakfast-cloths, and scarfs with doilies.

There should be napkins to match the nicer table-cloths, and it is desirable to have them match the more plebeian ones also, but this is not obligatory, as often bargains in napkins fall in one's way which it would be folly to miss because they do not match the cloth. Good napkins for children and ordinary use may be made from the partly worn table-cloths.

Often in the South, and a great deal through the North, table-cloths are used only for dinner and lunch, while for breakfast and supper or tea, small cloths, scarfs, or doilies are used, and there is hardly a more attractive sight than a table so set with handsome napery over shining mahogany.

Before putting on the table-cloth, the silence cloth should go on first, not only, as its name suggests, to prevent any objectionable noise from dishes or silver, but also to save the table from stains and scratches. This cloth may be of double-faced cotton flannel, knitted table padding, or an asbestos pad. The first two launder well and the last is easily handled when made in sections, and may be protected from soil by the use of linen covers which are made to fit the pads. A unique idea and an inexpensive one is to use sheets of corrugated cardboard in linen covers instead of the asbestos pads.

Over the silence cloth goes the table-cloth, which should hang nine inches or more below the edge of the table on all sides. A white linen centrepiece is sometimes used on the table-cloth, but this is not necessary.

When setting the table for luncheon or supper with doilies, the set should consist of a centrepiece, and plate, tumbler, and bread-and-butter plate doilies. The last two are sometimes omitted and only one doily, large enough to accommodate the entire individual service, substituted. The doilies may be round or square, in colors or all white, lace trimmed or all linen as the fancy may dictate and the conditions seem to require. The luncheon-cloth, which is perfectly correct to use for breakfast, luncheon, or supper, should reach just to the edge of the table or hang a few inches below it, and should be accompanied by the small luncheon napkins.

In hemming table linen, very narrow hems or the so-called French hem will do very nicely unless a hem-stitch is preferred, in which case a wider hem is used. The French hem is made by turning the hem in the usual way, then turning it back on itself on the right side of the linen, making the crease just where the stitches will come, and the hem is caught down by whipping the edge of the hem to the crease with fine stitches. When the hem is smoothed out the stitches will scarcely show at all.

When table linen is hemstitched the hem of the table-cloth should be an inch and a half or two inches wide and that on the napkins one-half to one inch, depending upon the size of the napkins.

The square tea-cloth and napkin illustrated below are simply orna-

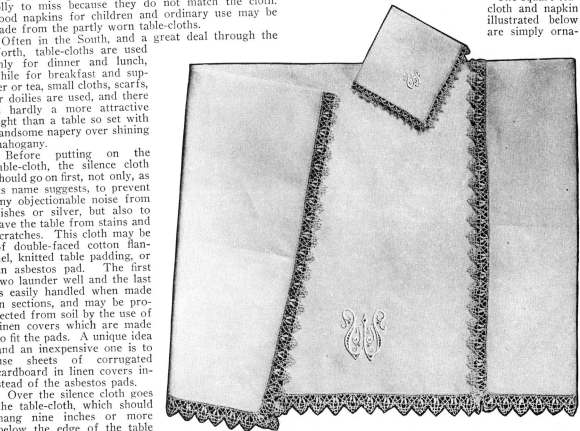

No. 16-1-5. LACE-TRIMMED TEA CLOTH AND NAPKIN WITH SINGLE ORNAMENTAL INITIAL FOR NAPKIN, 1¼-INCH; FOR CLOTH, 3½ INCHES

mented with a fine Cluny edge and a pretty initial in French and eyelet embroidery. In this instance the three-and-a-half-inch letter on the cloth is placed on the side instead of in the corner and the one-inch letter on the napkin is in the corner.

Sheets should be selected of ample size to cover the beds nicely and tuck under the mattress ten inches or more. These are finished with an inch hem at the bottom and a two or three inch hem at the top unless the upper sheet is embroidered with a scalloped edge. It is not necessary to hem the selvaged sides.

Pillow-cases should fit the pillows neatly, not being too large nor too small, and be finished with a two-inch hem or scallops. Besides the simple pillow-case which opens at one end, there is also the "day time" pillow-slip, which is made exactly like the ordinary slip except that it is open at both ends and is finished either with hems or scallops and may contain an embroidery design in the centre. The "envelope" slip is also popular for use during the day if one does not care for shams or scarfs. The envelope cases are made in the shape of a large envelope with a pointed, rounded, or square flap, which is finished with embroidered scallops or lace and also contains other embroidery, either sprays or a monogram.

In buying bed linen it should be done with circumspection, as the sizes of beds and pillows differ so greatly that it is necessary for every housekeeper to take her own measurements, which should be done with system so that one will not make the mistake of getting sizes which will be too cumbersome or will be scant when making up the bed.

No. 16-1-7. A 22-Inch Centrepiece, Lace Trimmed and Simply Embroidered

The white woven bedspreads are always in good taste, and the spreads made of plain linen hemmed or scalloped and embroidered with a monogram six or eight inches in height enclosed in a wreath are also popular. Some of the embroidered spreads are quite elaborate and contain cut-work, French and eyelet embroidery and other styles of stitches.

In selecting towels there should be a variety of sizes and textures, including large and small Turkish bath towels, huckaback in several sizes and qualities, and the finer, softer damask towels for special use when a very soft towel is needed.

The centrepiece No. 16-1-7 is quite simple in design and very pleasing. With it may be used doilies in two sizes, ten and seven inches, the entire set embroidered in the dots and semi-monogram, which of course is made smaller for the doilies. The edge as illustrated is finished with a fine Cluny lace buttonholed to the linen, but a crocheted or tatted edge would be as appropriate.

The centrepiece No. 15-4-44 is much more elaborate, as the entire edge is cut-work. This is done by running the edges, then buttonholing them very narrowly. As the lines are being run, the buttonholed bars are put in. To make the picots, carry the thread back, catch with a buttonhole loop into the fourth stitch from the last, then cover this loop with buttonholing and continue the bar or edge.

No. 15-4-44. A 25-Inch Centrepiece with Cut-Work Edge

No. 14-4-44. Five-Inch
Finger-Bowl Doily

T HE white luncheon-cloth on this page has some unusual little points aside from its general beauty. The cloth is full size for a fifty-four-inch round table, and it will be noticed that the French and eyelet pepper-berry design is four-sided. This design is planned so that the plates may be placed in the border in such a way that they will not cover any of the embroidery, and yet the design is not so decided that it would matter if six covers were laid instead of four. The cloth should be put on the table so that the initial will come at the left of the hostess. This style of initial may be seen in the larger illustration on page 7, No. 118.

It will be noticed that the fifteen-inch napkin, which matches this cloth, is also marked with an Old English letter, but being so much smaller it is impractical to try to work it with eyelets, so it is worked entirely in satin-stitch. It is not necessary to mark the little

five-inch finger-bowl doily with an initial, and yet, if desired, a tiny letter may be placed just to the right of the spray of berries and leaves between the scallops and the inner circle.

It may be well to mention that the large stem of the berries which forms the circle inside the

No. 14-4-45. Fifteen-Inch Napkin

lunch-cloth is composed of two lines of satin outlining with seed-stitches between. This makes a much more pleasing effect than a heavy band of solid embroidery and lends variety to the design without much additional work for the embroiderer.

No. 14-4-43. A 54-Inch Lunch Cloth in French and Eyelet Embroidery

Napkins and Napkin Cases

LITTLE hemstitched napkins, fifteen inches square, made of plain smooth linen and ornamented in the corners with an initial surrounded by a spray or wreath in fine French and eyelet embroidery are much used for breakfast, luncheon, and tea. The napkins may be procured already hemstitched and then ornamented to suit the fancy, or they may be hemmed by hand if one prefers to have the napkin all in hand work.

No. 13-9-65.   Tea Napkin

A single initial or small monogram without any other embroidery is always neat and in good taste, but the bit of design around the letter adds individuality and is very pleasing when well done. It is understood that any white embroidery on table linen must be carefully done to be of any account whatever.

space. The whole alphabet like this letter is shown in line on page 6. Besides being suitable for napkins, it is also appropriate for men's handkerchiefs, but no wreath is necessary on the handkerchief.

On the four napkins at the bottom of the page it will be noticed that the style of letter is chosen, in each case, to suit the design surrounding it. They are all in French embroidery with an occasional eyelet, and in these designs the work is padded closely, but not too heavily, and covered with very regular satin-stitches. A more open effect may be obtained by working the petals of the flowers as eyelets if one wishes to do this kind of work.

The two cases in the centre of the page are for

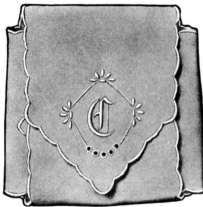
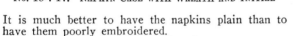

No. 15-7-17.   Napkin Case with Wreath and Initial

No. 15-7-21.   A Practical Case for Napkins

It is much better to have the napkins plain than to have them poorly embroidered.

A very fine needle and fine thread are necessary to accomplish perfect results in either French or eyelet embroidery, and this is especially true when the fabric is fine and smooth.

The napkin at the top of the page shows a very pleasing design in French and eyelet work with a very little seed stitching. The long slim letter is in satin-outline and is most satisfactory in this particular

napkins, simply to be folded over and not fastened, unless snap fasteners are put under the upper flap, and they are also useful as hot-roll cases, or for biscuit, muffins, or toast. The first case shows a very conventional wreath surrounding an Old English initial. This motif is quite suitable for towels or pillow-cases, or for small tea-cloths.

These cases are all complete when the embroidery is finished, as they require no putting together. They are made of squares of white linen with the corners cut

No. 14-11-61

No. 14-11-64

No. 14-11-65

No. 14-11-66

Luncheon Napkins Marked with Initials and Wreaths all in White Embroidery out and the edges scalloped. On the case No. 15-7-21 the wreath of French and eyelet embroidery encloses a Japanese letter of suitable size. The letter should be padded quite heavily, then worked smoothly in satin-stitch. This design is also suitable for many other purposes if one wishes a simple wreath which may be easily worked.

The violet and cosmos designs at the top of the page are made to enclose the long narrow letter mentioned before, and this not only fits nicely into the space, but also harmonizes well with the slender stems of the flowers and is worked in the same way that the stems are worked. Single lines such as these are worked in satin-outline and there are several ways of doing this as is suggested in the first part of the book among the stitches. Some workers prefer one method and some another.

The solid parts of the embroidery are worked by first padding the space evenly, letting the stitches run lengthwise of the design, then covering closely with satin-stitch. As has been said before, to make nice eyelets, a very fine needle and fine thread are necessary and the stitches must be short and regular.

The design of No. 13-9-64 consists almost entirely of eyelets; only the Old English letter and flower petals are worked solid. When eyelets are close together as these are, care must be taken to keep them all perfectly round, and this is best

done by first running all the eyelets by carrying the thread on the upper edge of one and the lower edge of the next all around the ring and then reversing the operation when the thread is brought back. Begin to whip the first eyelet at the point nearest the next one, then, before cutting the second eyelet, run the thread half around it so as to begin next to the third, and so on. This makes it easy to go from the finished eyelet to the next without fastening the thread.

In the grape and daisy design larger designs are also shown for tea-cloths. These may be embroidered on the hemstitched squares or on regular table-cloths as the wreaths are of a suitable size for either. Enlarged designs may also be had to match all the other napkin designs on these two pages.

These dainty little motifs are very pleasing for embroidering household linens and are preferred by some to the more elaborate all-over effects. The edges of the linen may be simply hemmed or finished with scallops and then the initial which is to mark it is enclosed within an attractive floral or conventional wreath and this is all the ornament necessary.

The designs shown on these two pages are suitable and appropriate for almost any household or personal articles and the suggestions they contain will be useful for all kinds of marking, as they can be adapted and changed to suit different needs.

No. 14-6-46

No. 14-6-47

TEA OR LUNCHEON NAPKINS

No. 14-6-48. GRAPE NAPKIN

No. 14-6-49. COSMOS NAPKIN

No. 13-9-64. WITH RING OF EYELETS

No. 14-6-50 GRAPE TEA CLOTH

No. 14-6-51 COSMOS TEA CLOTH

No. 13-9-66. IN JAPANESE DESIGN

Towels in Various Styles

No. 15-7-13. Towel Strap

NOWADAYS there are at least two sizes of towels in every supply of household linens, the regulation towel measuring about twenty-two by forty inches and the small hand or guest towel measuring about sixteen by twenty-seven inches. The little guest towel, while not fully appreciated by every one, came to fill a real need. Our laundry, so often overfull anyway, has added to it a towel used by a guest once; if it be a small one, it means just so much less time spent in washing and ironing it, so these towels are both useful and economical, as well as dainty and pretty.

While there are a variety of fancy huckabacks to be had, there is, after all, nothing more satisfactory than the plain, firmly woven fabric ornamented with hand embroidery. Of course on a towel both sides of the embroidery are in evidence, so the worker must be very careful to have the wrong side of the embroidery look quite as well as the right.

Heavily raised satin embroidery is always in good taste for towels, but for the many who like a variety,

colored embroidery may also be used in satin-stitch, cross-stitch or darning.

Towel straps of linen such as the one shown at the top of the page are especially useful in storing away towels in the linen closet. With tape attached to each end, the straps may be tied around a number of towels to keep them in order.

The towel No. 15-7-57 is full size and is ornamented with a rose wreath enclosing an Old English initial. The ribbon and petals of the roses are worked in satin-stitch and the centres of the flowers have little woven wheels made with the needle. At the top of the hem is a narrow band of drawn-work.

Nos. 15-9-21 and 15-7-16 are both guest towels, one having scalloped ends and the other finished with hemstitched hems. Both are embroidered all in white

No. 15-7-16. The Daisies Make a Pretty Enclosure for the Script Initial

in padded satin-stitch.

The towels Nos. 13-11-51 and 52 besides having initials enclosed in ornamental wreaths also have borders of Oriental drawn-work just above the hems. This work is effective and easily executed, and is especially charming when developed in some soft pastel shade with white.

In preparing the border of No. 13-11-51 two inches from the bottom, draw threads seven-eighths of an inch in depth. It is not necessary to hemstitch the sides of this drawn space, but the weaving is done over and under four or five threads of the warp. Four

No. 15-7-57. Old English Letter in an Embroidered Wreath

dence, so the worker must be very careful to have the wrong side of the embroidery look quite as well as the right.

Heavily raised satin embroidery is always in good taste for towels, but for the many who like a variety,

No. 13-11-51. This Conventional Wreath is Good for Table Linens

No. 15-9-21. Satin-Stitch and Solid Embroidery all in White. This Design is also Suitable for Pillow Cases

threads of stranded cotton or a coarser thread is used for this work. In commencing the pattern, begin with the colored thread and leave the end of the thread to be run in later. With a blunt tapestry needle, weave in and out, over and under four or five threads of the warp for each group until eight groups are covered. Weave back and forth until one-fourth of the space is filled, eight rows. Now omit each outside group and weave six groups eight times; drop end groups and weave four groups eight times; drop end groups and weave two groups eight times. This completes the first colored figure. Run the thread down through the finished figure and work the next colored figure, and so on to the end. The first white figure is never entire. Begin at the widest part and weave the three groups eight times, two groups eight times, then wrap the last group eight times. For

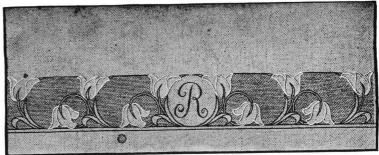

No. 15-9-10. THE BACKGROUND OF DARNING BRINGS OUT THE DESIGN

figures alternate all the way across the end of the towel.

The towel in darning, No. 15-9-10, is worked in two shades of yellow and two of green, using three threads of stranded cotton which slips easily under the small threads of the huckaback. The outer petals of the tulips are darned and outlined with light yellow and the centre petal is darker yellow; the stems and leaves are outlined in green and the background is darned with a darker green, which is also used for outlining the edges of the bands and the hem.

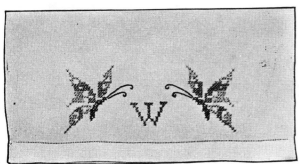

No. 15-8-15. BUTTERFLIES IN CROSS-STITCH

the entire white figures, weave six groups eight times, four groups eight times, and two groups eight times. Always run in the loose ends of threads to finish off.

For the border of No. 13-11-52 leave two inches for the hem and draw the threads for five-eighths of an inch. With colored thread weave eight groups four times, six groups four times, four groups four times, two groups seven times or to fill space. The half figure at the beginning is colored like the first whole one and is made with the same thread. Weave three seven times, two four times, and wrap one four times.

Weave the large white figure exactly as the whole colored figure was woven, then go on with the small white figure, weave six seven times, four four times, and two four times. These white and colored

No. 16-1-10. THIS LETTER NEEDS NO WREATH OF FLOWERS

The butterfly towel is in cross-stitch in colors, dull blue and yellow being the principal colors employed.

The other two towels on the page speak for themselves, the upper one has a single initial in fancy script, the other being ornamented with a floral design and an irregular edge.

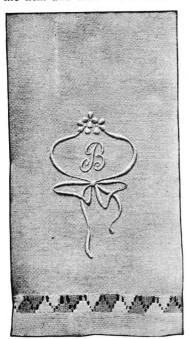

No. 13-11-52. THE BOW-KNOT AND SCRIPT LETTER ARE EASY TO WORK

No. 15-9-19. A SCALLOPED END THAT IS UNUSUAL. THE SPACE AT THE CENTRE IS JUST RIGHT FOR A LINE INITIAL

Bureau Covers

IT is in good taste to make scarfs or covers for all pieces of furniture, and the linens which are intended to cover just the tops may be made to fit exactly, each piece individual as it were. This requires thoughtful measuring and planning, but looks more careful and artistic and is prettier than a cover which must be either folded back or fails to cover the furniture upon which it is placed.

repeating the corner and central figure, which are perfectly symmetrical. This design, with its open eyelets, will look pretty over any dark furniture. The space in the middle of the front is especially designed for an initial.

The cover at the bottom of the page is elaborate in work because the lace line is really a Venetian point worked into the linen, but a linen Cluny lace may be

No. 14-7-2. SIDEBOARD SCARF IN FRENCH AND EYELET EMBROIDERY, WITH SPACE ARRANGED
FOR A 3-INCH LETTER

The sides and front of bureau-covers are usually all that are worked, the edge of the back being finished with a narrow hem, and where the embroidery and hem meet, the scalloping should not be finished at the corner until the hem has been turned and then the embroidery is done over the hem to make it quite complete and neat.

The cover at the top of the page may be used either for a sideboard or bureau, and the pattern may easily be adapted for a square tea-cloth or stand-cover by

used in place of this with perfectly good effect.

The pincushion is in mattress form, having an upper and lower section and a side section connecting the two. It is stuffed with lamb's wool and tightly tufted.

The last charming touch to be given to linens of this sort is the monogram. A little one may be placed on the pincushion and a larger one towards the front edge of the scarf. This of course makes the linen more personal, and as a gift a little more attractive. This very pleasing monogram is shown larger on page 16.

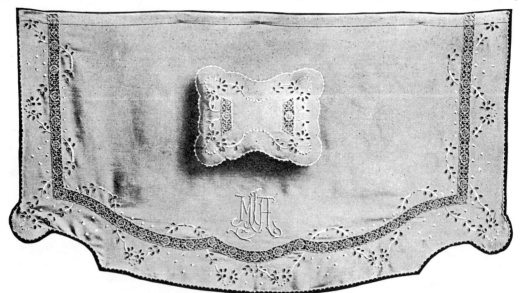

No. 13-11-12. PINCUSHION   No. 13-11-13. SCARF
MONOGRAM NO. 14-1-12, PAGE 16, IS USED ON THE SCARF, AND IN SMALLER SIZE MAY
ALSO BE EMBROIDERED ON THE PINCUSHION

Sheets and Pillow Slips

EMBROIDERED pillow-cases, sheets, and towels add very much to the feeling of careful furnishing in the bedroom, and often the embroidery takes the form of a medallion or wreath surrounding the monogram or initial. This gives a more elaborate look, not only because it is elaborate, but because it centres the attention on the decoration and apparently pulls it together as it were.

No. 13-9-18. SUITABLE FOR BOTH PILLOW CASE AND SHEET

The two upper designs on this page are shown one on a pillow-case and one on a towel, but both designs are suitable for both articles and can also be used on sheets to make a complete set. The daisy wreath in No. 14-11-46 can be made in various sizes and used on all the household linen for both dining-room and bedroom. This makes an attractive spot, and is sufficient decoration if a pretty scallop is used on the edges. A script or Japanese letter may be substituted for the Old English initial and the effect will be equally as good.

The design No. 13-9-14 carrying the punched-work ribbon is particularly attractive and would still be good if the punched work were omitted and seed-stitches or some fancy lace stitch used instead, or the ribbon can be simply outlined without spoiling the design.

No. 14-11-46. EMBROIDERED GUEST TOWEL

The more elaborate design No. 13-9-15 is one of the daintiest patterns that can be imagined for bridal linen. Not only are the wreaths and festoons ornamental, but the letters themselves are very decorative and fit in harmoniously with the rest of the design. As may be seen from the illustration, the principal stitches employed here are the seed-stitch and satin-stitch with some satin outlining.

When sheets, pillow-cases, and towels are hemmed and hand-embroidered, it is better to have the hemstitching done by hand, as this seems more in keeping than to have the hems made by machine, and there is a certain satisfaction in knowing that all the stitchery is handwork.

A very pretty and substantial method of finishing the ends of bed linen is to first make a wide hem, hemstitched or not as preferred, and then embroider a deep scallop near the edge through both thicknesses of linen and trim away the linen outside the scallops in the usual way. This makes a firm end which is also pleasing in appearance, and with it only a very simple embroidery design is needed; a single monogram is sufficient.

No. 13-9-14. SHEET. THE SHAMROCK WREATH IS NICE EVEN WITHOUT THE RIBBON

No. 13-9-15. A GOOD DESIGN FOR BRIDAL SHEETS AND PILLOW CASES

An Attractive Medallion for Enclosing an Initial

No. 15-1-24, Pincushion, and Bureau Scarf No. 15-1-25

THE medallion design on these two pages runs through the entire set of bedroom linen without becoming monotonous. All the articles are embroidered in white with the exception of the little towel, which is in two shades of blue. The shaded eyelets and outside line of the oval are in the light blue, and the dots, leaves, stems, and inner line are in the darker shade. Of course, if one prefers, the towel may be worked in white like the other pieces.

On the hemstitched bureau-cover the medallion with its Old English initial forms the entire decoration and is very pleasing. The little oval pincushion is as dainty and pretty a bit of embroidery as one could desire and forms a real ornament for the dresser. The top cover is buttonholed in fine scallops on the edge and contains a medallion with an initial and eyelets for lacing, while the bottom cover is worked only with the eyelets, the edge being finished with lace.

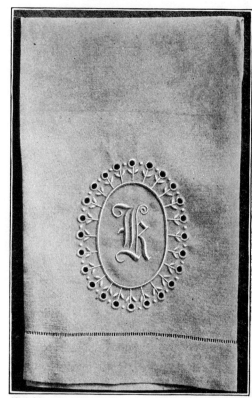

No. 15-1-22. Pillow Case with Double Hemstitching

Pillow-cases and sheets are made to match, and if shams or a scarf should be preferred to the pillow-cases, the sheet medallion may be used. While any single letter can be used in these medallions, the Old English initial as illustrated seems the most appropriate with this particular style of design. It is always a safe style to use on household linens especially if they are finished with hemstitched borders.

In working the shaded eyelets they are padded on the heavy side as for French embroidery and run in the usual way on the narrow side, then the opening is cut and shaped and the eyelet whipped very carefully and evenly. The leaves and dots are in satin-stitch and the stems and oval in satin outline. The towel is an exception to this as two lines of simple outline are used for the oval.

The usual width for pillow-cases is twenty-two inches, and they are made long enough to cover the pillow nicely without too much superfluous end to hang over and look untidy. They should be just long enough to show the embroidery nicely if the end is embroidered, and the proper

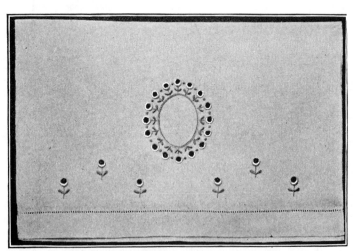

No. 15-1-23. Hemstitched Huckaback Guest Towel

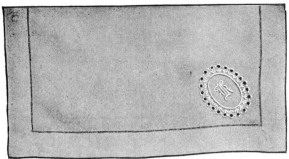

No. 15-1-20. STAND COVER

the design is nice to use on a made-up spread if one with a plain centre can be procured.

In working the ring of small eyelets surrounding the letter, it is better not to fasten off the thread after each eyelet, but to let it run from the finished eyelet to the next one to be worked. Care must be taken in embroidering the letter to keep the lines straight and regular and to have padding of the same thickness throughout. When well done this design is intensely pleasing, and it must be well done to be at all satisfactory.

A set of bedroom linens which match or which are decorated in a uniform manner in some simple restful design are lovely and quiet in a sleeping-room. The effect is so much better than where the covers, bedspread, and other hangings are varied and different. In the first place a white bed is after all the prettiest. Openwork and lace spreads with color under them do not have so restful an effect, and are not always in such good taste as the simple white hemstitched and embroidered linen spread with the white embroidered pillow cases or scarf; and another point in favor of the white hangings is that they are easily laundered.

length must of course be gauged by the size of the pillows themselves, which are made in various sizes.

The usual size of sheets for double beds is ninety inches wide by ninety-nine inches long; for single beds they are the same length, but only seventy-two inches wide. They may be even narrower still for the thirty-six-inch beds. As has been stated before, only the top sheet is ornamented, the bottom one being finished with plain hems.

The hemstitched standcover at the top of the page is ornamented with a single medallion in one corner, and this contains the same initial which is used on the other pieces. This square may be in any size to fit the top of the lamp-stand or it can hang over the edges. The favorite sizes for this purpose are twenty-four, thirty, and thirty-six inches. The medallion may be used on an even larger square for a tea-cloth or table-cover, for the design is equally as appropriate for the dining-room as for the bedroom.

The large oval for the bedspread is twelve inches high and the letter is five inches. Two-inch letters are used on all the other designs in this set except the towel where the letter is one and one-half inches. This design for a bedspread is embroidered on the spread so that it will come in the centre of the mattress when the spread is on the bed, and the base of the letter is towards the foot of the bed. The spread may be made of plain linen sheeting hemstitched on all four sides if it is to match the other pieces in the set, or buttonholed in scallops if it is to be used alone; or

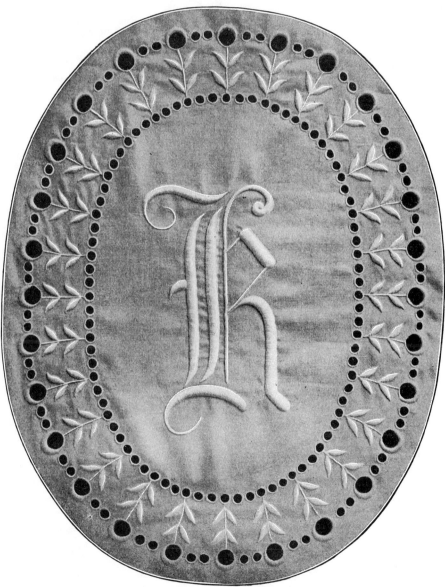

No. 15-1-21. DESIGN FOR DECORATING BEDSPREAD

Bedroom Set Marked with Monograms

IN arranging the bed covering a very unique and convenient plan is to have the pillow or bolster roll button on to the spread. This arrangement is much more satisfactory than having the roll-cover and spread all in one piece as is sometimes done, for the two parts are much easier to handle than one im-

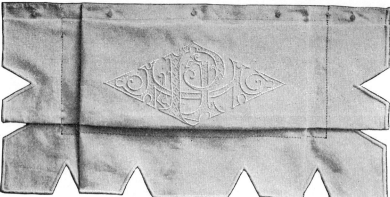

pillow - roll by varying its shape to suit the shape of the scarf. A pair of monograms, one square and the other oblong, thus matching each other, makes a beautiful centre decoration for both the spread and the pillow-scarf.

The initial of the surname is the most prominent and comes

mense piece. The plain edge of the roll-sham is buttoned to the top edge of the spread, then it slips under the roll, comes over on top and the scalloped edge lies on the spread.

If the stiff cardboard bolster-form is used, it may have openings in the back and the night pillows stuffed into the form during the day. This keeps the rumpled pillows out of sight and yet in a very convenient place for use when they are needed.

A bedspread, although a large piece of work, may be quite simple. A large monogram is sufficient decoration, and the same monogram should be used on the

in the centre of the design with the other letters arranged across or on each side as the particular letters seem to work in best, for as no two sets of letters can be arranged in exactly the same manner, each monogram is a study in itself.

In working this style of monogram, it is always a good idea to embroider the large centre letter in a different manner from the other two letters, because in this way it shows much more distinctly. The different style of work separates it and throws it out from the other letters. In all these letters a line of closely laid work outlines them on both sides and the fancy stitches

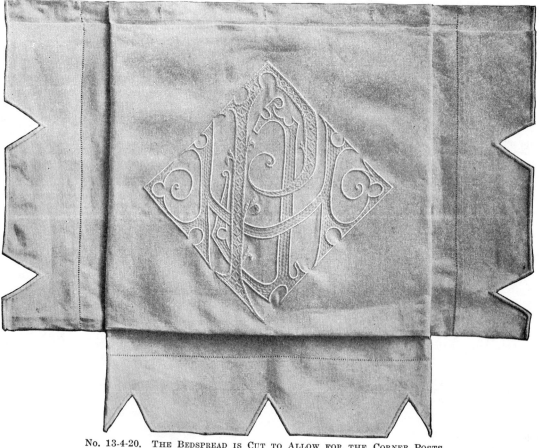

No. 13-4-20. THE BEDSPREAD IS CUT TO ALLOW FOR THE CORNER POSTS

34

No. 14-8-24. SMALL COVER FOR OLD-FASHIONED BUREAU
WITH SIDE DRAWERS

No. 14-8-22. THE INITIAL OF THE SURNAME IS USED IN THE
MIDDLE BECAUSE IT SHOULD BE THE MOST PROMINENT
LETTER IN A MONOGRAM, AND SHOULD CATCH THE EYE
FIRST

or seeding are filled in between the satin outlines.

If the bed is beautiful old mahogany, the cover should not hang over very much, but on the simple brass beds it is well to let the sides and ends come within a few inches of the floor, especially if no valance is used, and none is necessary with the spread here shown.

It will be noticed from the illustrations that the scarf and spread are finished with a wide hem besides the cleft scallop, and while this hem is not absolutely necessary, it gives a firm border and also an ornamental finish to the linen. The hem should be turned about one inch wider than it is to be when finished in order to give sufficient edge to hold in working the edge. The double hemstitching should be done first and then the edge run with rather heavy padding and covered with close firm buttonholing, using a coarse embroidery cotton.

The little toilet-table cover, No. 13-4-18, matches the spread and scarf and contains a smaller square monogram at the middle of one side. The linen and cotton for working should both be finer for this than for the

spread. The design of this edge may be carried out on the towels for the room if one likes and on one or two lingerie slumber pillows. The same edge and monogram are also suitable for a bureau-scarf, and a smaller monogram may be used on the pincushion.

No. 14-8-22 shows this monogram worked in a dif-

No. 14-8-23. PINCUSHION COVER LACED TOGETHER OVER A
MATTRESS CUSHION

ferent manner, but one which is equally as pleasing as the preceding. Here the middle letter of the design is in cut-work, which is always effective, and the others are in padded satin-stitch. This cut-work letter is very beautiful and ornamental when used alone, and there is a detail of it in process of working on page 5.

The little oblong bureau cover, which may be used for any odd piece of furniture, and the pincushion on this page show this monogram used as it is and also adapted to a diamond shape, either of which is very pleasing and suitable for many varieties of household linen.

The oblong pincushion-cover is laced together over a silk or satin-covered mattress form, which should be made to exactly fit, allowing the satin covering to show around the sides between the lacing. The back of the cover is the same shape as the top, but it has no ornament other than the buttonholed edge and the eyelets for lacing.

The straight scallops used on all these articles are easy to embroider.

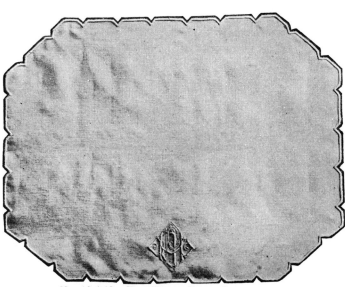

No. 13-4-18. THE TOILET-TABLE LINEN COVER

IN marking little cases, often a pretty monogram is all the decoration that is necessary. This forms a neat, attractive spot on an otherwise plain surface which is very pleasing in its decorative effect. Some good examples of this ornamentation are given on this and the following page, and these particular monograms are also useful for many other purposes; in fact, for any other purpose for which this style of marking is required.

At the centre of the page is shown a doily-case for ten-inch doilies, and below at the left is a smaller case in the same design for seven-inch doilies. In making these cases four circles of linen are required, or two circles of linen and two of some different material for the lining. The monogram is first embroidered on the linen, which is then pressed very smooth and the circles cut half an inch larger than the cardboard. Run a gathering thread around the edge of each circle of linen and fit it on to a circle of the cardboard, then whip two covered pieces together very neatly on the edges and cover the edges with a fine cord to hide the sewing of the linen.

The ribbons are arranged on the top sec-

No. 13-8-6. Sizes, 2 and 3 Inches, Including Height of Entire Design

No. 13-8-11.
Doily Case

tion simply for decorative purposes, the real hinges consisting of narrow tapes or strips of linen fastened between the back and front. The ribbon hinges are plainly seen in the other doily-case, No. 15-4-60, which is made in the same manner as the ones just described, except the decoration, which in this case consists of a single initial enclosed in a wreath of daisies and leaves with a conventional line extending around inside the circle. Although the illustration is small, this case is for twelve-inch doilies.

The monogram, or rather the three letters enclosed within three circles at the top of the page, is practically the same that is used on two of the doily-cases. In this larger illustration, one may easily see the style of embroidery, which is the same satin-stitch which enters so largely into monogram work. In working these block letters, care must be taken to keep them true to the drawing, and to have the lines firm and regular, and especial care must be taken with the circles to keep them circles. For an open effect the leaves may readily be worked as eyelets which are very pleasing when used over dark furniture or a color.

No. 13-8-10. Doily Case

No. 15-4-60. Doily Case

Simple Cases for Men

THE set of shirt, glove, and necktie cases is designed especially for men to use in a suit-case. They are made of linen, preferably the natural color, or tan linen of regular weave, but may be of white if desired, and may be lined or not as one likes.

The shirt-case for evening shirts is made like a long narrow envelope, but it has a two-inch strip inserted on each side to form hinges and give it depth. If the case is intended to hold several shirts the hinges should be wider. It is left open at the top and bottom, as it is rather easier to slip the shirts in than if it is closed at the bottom. This is really a very useful device for keeping the shirts unrumpled in a suit-case, and is an article which every man who travels at all should appreciate. Women will also find it useful as a shirt-waist case, making it perhaps a trifle shorter.

The glove-case, which may also be used for handkerchiefs, is another practical article, and one which is easily made. It is in one piece of linen which simply folds over and forms the case when it is folded and buttoned.

The necktie-case is similar to the glove-case, but is longer and fastens with two buttons. If the cases are lined they are piped with white, and bias muslin may

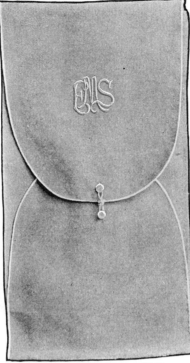

No. 13-8-7.   SHIRT CASE

be used for this purpose. If preferred, the bias muslin may be used over a cord, which is then inserted in the same way in which piping is secured. This makes a very pretty and substantial-looking finish, and helps to keep the cases well in shape. If they are not lined, the edges are bound with bias bands.

The very simple, pleasing monogram used on these cases is quite suitable for any other purpose, and is good in almost any size. It is also legible and easy to embroider. One cannot make a mistake in working this if ordinary care is exercised in the em-

broidery, for only one stitch is employed, the familiar satin-stitch, and the letters themselves are of such an easy, graceful character that they are not at all difficult to follow.

This monogram is also nice for household linens of every kind and may be used on wearing apparel with perfectly good effect if it is made in a suitable size. There are quite a number of articles which may be marked for men besides these particular cases, and all hearsay to the contrary, the majority of men like pretty things as well as the average woman does. Their shirts and pajamas may be marked, also handkerchiefs, mufflers, collar-bags, laundry-bags, chiffonier-covers, pincushions and other personal bedroom linens.

In making the cases shown on this page it is not necessary to be restricted to the particular monogram here illustrated, for there are numberless other designs which are equally as appropriate and which might please some fancies even better than these. A conventional monogram enclosed within a decorative wreath or a single initial so enclosed may be used, or even the initial alone is not bad if an attractive one is chosen.

It will be noticed that the fasteners on these cases are buttons and loops. The buttons are made of little wooden molds covered with the same linen which is used for the cases, and the cord is a tightly twisted mercerized cotton cord. If preferred, pretty pearl buttons may be used, or the buttons and loops may be dispensed with entirely and the flaps fastened down with snap fasteners. When making up articles of this character the greatest care must be exercised in every particular of the work to keep it professional-like, neat

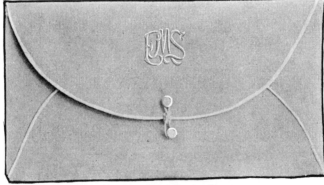

No. 13-8-8.   GLOVE CASE

and well finished. It is the little points which make the work more choice and careful and constitute the real beauty of hand-needlework.

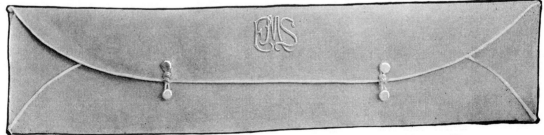

No. 13-8-9.   NECKTIE CASE.   MOST SUITABLE AND USEFUL ARTICLE FOR A MAN

CROCHETED INITIALS

THE SAME DESIGNS BEING SUITABLE FOR CROSS STITCH

ONE of the prettiest and most popular methods of marking linen at the present time is with crocheted initials set into the linen after the manner of a medallion, or worked into a crocheted band which is being used as an insertion. Many of the guest-towels, as well as those of larger sizes, are trimmed with crocheted insertion and edging, and when the crocheting is of the filet style, it is an easy matter to introduce a single initial or a group of initials. Monograms in filet crochet are more difficult to work so that they will be decipherable.

Any one who is at all familiar with the crochet-hook can easily do filet crochet, as very few stitches are necessary, and the directions are quite easy to understand and follow. The few brief rules and definitions which are necessary are as follows: A chain-stitch (ch) is made by drawing a loop through the loop already on the hook; treble crochet (t), having loop on hook, thread over, insert hook in work and draw thread through, thread over and draw through two loops, thread over and draw through remaining two loops.

A space consists of two chain-stitches below and above with a treble crochet on each side. A block consists of four treble crochet together; 2 blocks, 7 t; 3 blocks, 10 t, etc., always three times as many t plus one as there are blocks.

In making a chain to begin a piece of filet crochet, chain three times as

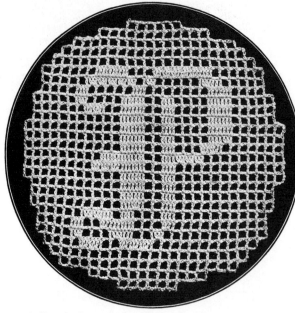

A SINGLE INITIAL CROCHETED IN MEDALLION EFFECT

No. 160. CROCHETED PINCUSHION COVER WITH THREE INITIALS

many stitches plus 1 as there are spaces, then if the first space is an open mesh, ch 5 to turn; if the row begins with a block, ch 3 to turn.

The letter P, which is crocheted within a circle, is from the alphabet on page 40, and is suitable to use on towels, pillow-cases, sheets, and lunch-cloths.

Begin with a chain of 24 stitches (st), t in 9th st from hook, (ch 2 miss 2, t in next st). Repeat until there are 6 spaces, which form the 1st row. *2d row*—Chain 14, t in 9th st from hook, ch 2, miss 2, t in next t, (ch 2, miss 2, t in top of t). Repeat across. To add the open spaces on the end of the row, ch 2, long treble (lt) (thread over 3 times) in same place last t was made, (ch 2, lt in middle of last lt) twice. The *3d row* is made the same as the 2d. For the *4th row*, ch 8 to begin and add one space at the end.

The letter is begun in the *5th row*, and is worked according to the block pattern. It may be well to draw the letter on cross section paper with the outline of the circle before beginning the crocheting.

The pincushion-top is plain filet crochet with loops of chain-stitches and balls around the edge, and is mounted over a colored satin form with ribbon puffed around the sides.

The insertion at the bottom of the page is very easy to crochet from the illustration, as it has straight edges and needs no especial explanation. For pillow-cases it is well to begin with the narrow part of the inser-

FILET CROCHET INSERTION WITH ONE INITIAL FOR PILLOW CASES, TOWELS, AND SHEETS

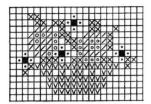

/ Light Rose   x Green
o Blue   . Deep Rose
■ Yellow   V Ecru

DIAGRAM SHOWING THE PLACING OF COLORS IN CROSS-STITCH BASKET ON TOWEL

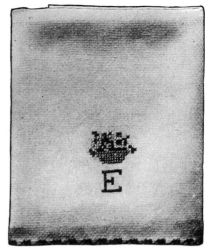

TOWEL WITH CROSS-STITCH BASKET AND INITIAL IN COLORS

tion, and when the initial is reached the width is increased by chaining a sufficient number of stitches for the extra spaces. After the initial is completed the insertion is diminished to the original width, making enough of the narrow part to extend around the pillow-case.

In making insertion for a sheet or towel, it is better to crochet the initial first and work the insertion both ways from it.

For the narrow part, commence with a chain of 33 st, t in 9th st from hook, ch 2, miss 2, t in next st. Repeat for open meshes and fill in with trebles for solid blocks. Any letter may be substituted for the M; one of the letters may be used from the alphabet on page 40, although they are larger than the one here illustrated, and will make the middle a little wider.

To insert the lace, narrowly hem both edges of the linen and whip both edges of the insertion in place, all except the initial, which will overlap one side of the linen. Carefully whip the edges of this in place and cut the linen underneath, leaving a narrow margin to turn back into a hem.

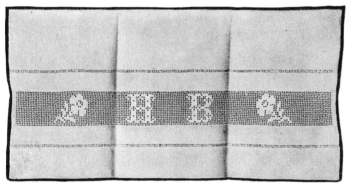

NO. 13-9-20. TOWEL BAND WITH INITIALS CROCHETED INTO THE DESIGN

The two towels on this page, with crocheted insertion, have the initials worked into the middle of the band with a floral design on each side, both designs making very attractive ends. It is quite an easy matter to regulate the length of the insertion No. 13-9-20, as so much of it consists of plain meshes, but in making No. 15-7-58, one must be careful to use rather fine crochet cotton, 70 or 80, and crochet so that the work will come 8 meshes to the inch, then the band will come about 26 inches long. If it is desired shorter, some of the end may be left off.

The little cross-stitch design, in colors, is very attractive on a guest-towel, and it may also be used on a bureau-cover and pincushion. This design is not stamped, but is worked from the diagram at the top of the page. It is worked over Penelope canvas which has first been basted on the linen, making a cross for every one of the symbols and using the color indicated by the symbol, then when the crosses are all fin-ished, the canvas is drawn away thread by thread, leaving the design on the linen. The letter is worked in blue. The end of the towel is narrowly turned once and finished with a simple crocheted edge worked into the huckaback. This consists of double crochet with 4-chain picots at regular intervals.

Any of the filet designs shown on these pages, and the alphabet on the next page, may be carried out in cross-stitch if one so desires. The rose pattern at the bottom of the page would be especially attractive in cross-stitch in rose colors and greens, and it is suitable for a number of purposes besides towel-ends.

A very beautiful bedspread can be crocheted from the design No. 15-7-58 by using carpet warp for the crocheted bands and joining them with linen strips. If the design is used in this way, the spray of roses should be repeated over and over without reversing, letting the design run continuously in one direction, until the strip is of the necessary length.

If desired, initials may be crocheted into the middle strip one above the other with the bases of the letters towards the foot of the bed, and these can be introduced in place of one of the rose repeats.

The linen strips may be either plain or embroidered, but with such a decorative design for the crocheting no embroidery is really necessary, unless one wished one of the strips to contain the embroidered initials.

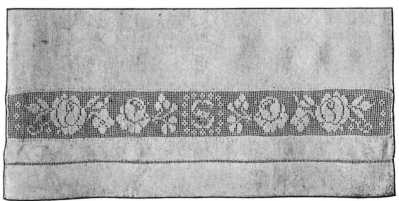

NO. 15-7-58. FILET CROCHET FOR MARKING AND TRIMMING

BLOCK ALPHABET FOR FILET CROCHET AND CROSS-STITCH

19 meshes high

IT must be remembered in working cross-stitch over canvas or directly by the weave of the material that the size of the mesh or the weave will determine the size of the whole design and one must plan accordingly.

The same principle holds in filet crochet; the coarser the thread and the looser the work the larger the work will come when finished. If one of the above initials is made with carpet warp and the meshes come four to the inch, the initial will be nearly five inches high; while if it is crocheted with No. 80 crochet cotton with the meshes eight to the inch, the letter will be exactly half as high.

If it is desired to make a letter a certain height, it is a good plan before commencing it to experiment with different threads, see how many meshes they crochet to the inch and estimate the size the letter will come. The crocheting of different workers varies.

40

MONOGRAM ALPHABETS FOR TRACING

BY TAKING ONE LETTER FROM EACH ALPHABET
THE THREE LETTERS MAY BE ARRANGED IN A CIRCLE

LETTERS ARRANGED WITHIN A CIRCLE

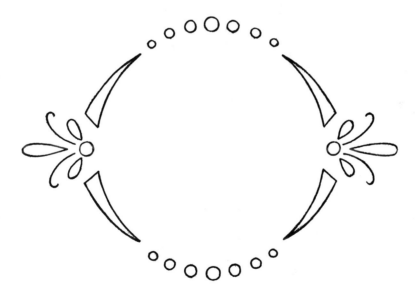

ORNAMENTAL CIRCLE FOR ENCLOSING THREE LETTERS

TO USE THE ALPHABETS THAT FOLLOW, TRACE THE THREE DESIRED LETTERS IN THEIR CORRECT RELATIVE
POSITIONS ON TRACING PAPER TO FORM A CIRCLE, AND TRANSFER TO THE LINEN WITH CARBON PAPER

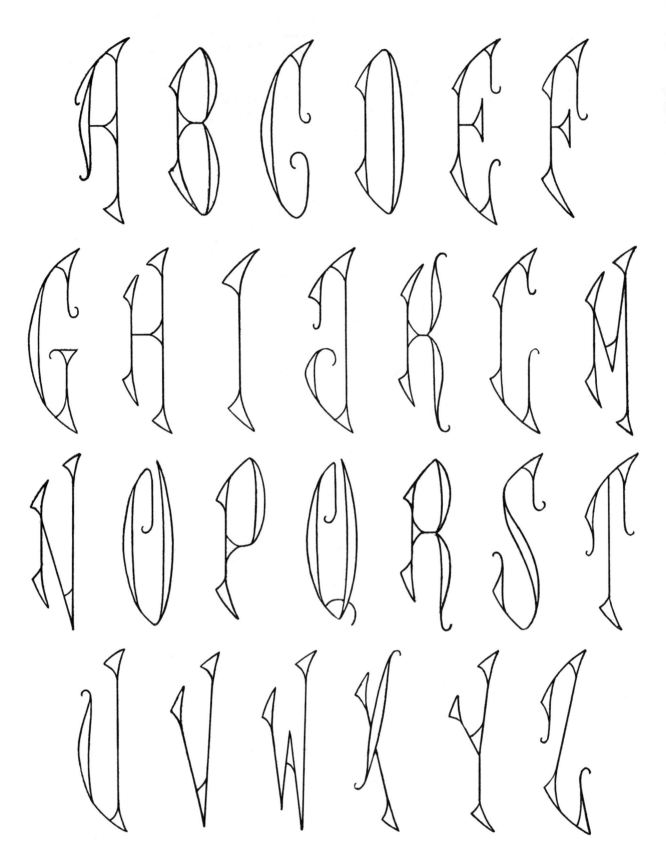

ALPHABET FOR LEFT OF GROUP. USE INITIAL OF FIRST NAME

42

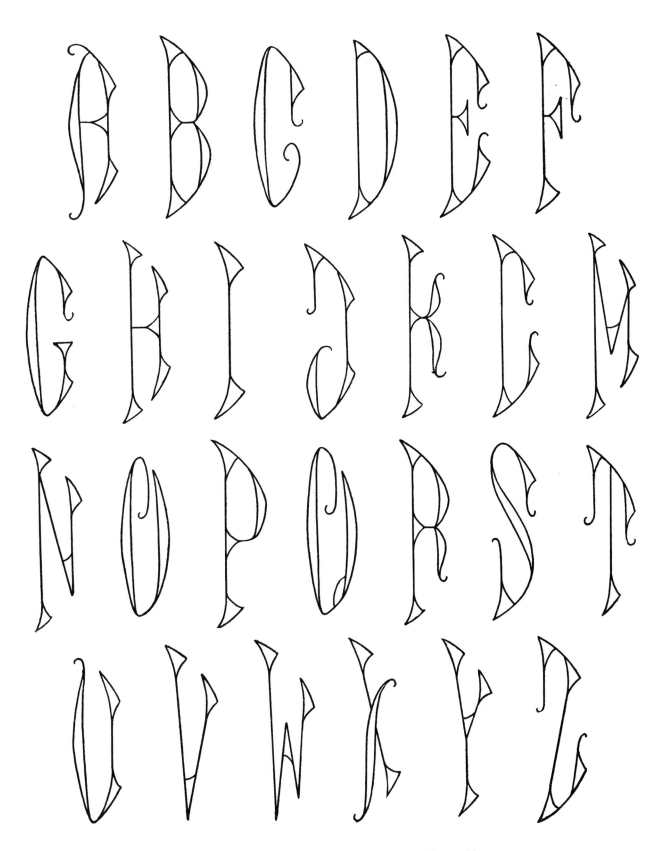

ALPHABET FOR RIGHT OF GROUP. USE INITIAL OF MIDDLE NAME

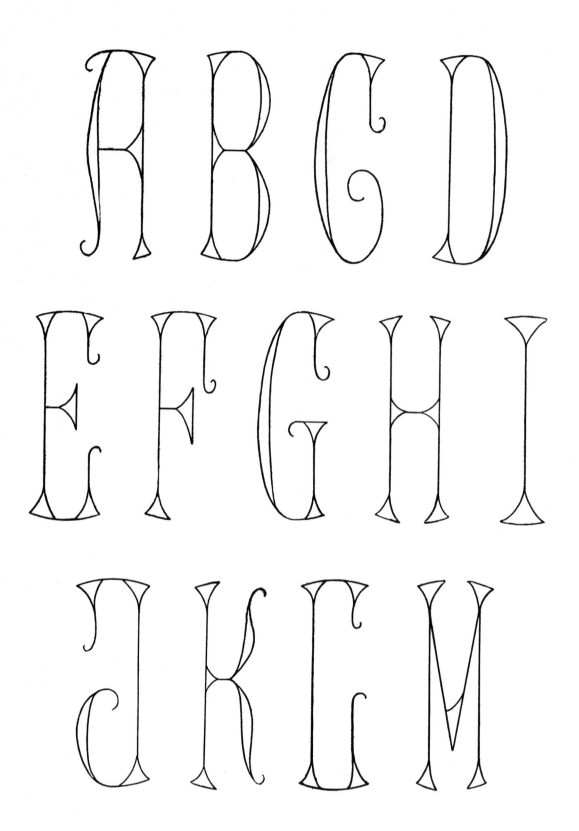

ALPHABET FOR MIDDLE OF GROUP. USE INITIAL OF SURNAME

44

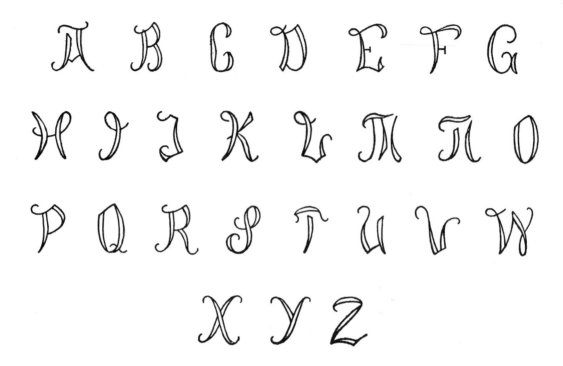

A Simple Alphabet Suitable for Handkerchiefs